Introduction to Literature

SYLVIA HUNT AND CYNTHIA PARR

Introduction to Literature
Planning and Teaching a First-year Course

Universitas Press
Montreal

Universitas Press
Montreal

www.universitaspress.com

First published in March 2019

Library and Archives Canada Cataloguing in Publication

Title: Introduction to literature : planning and teaching a first-year course /
   Sylvia Hunt & Cynthia Parr.
Names: Hunt, Sylvia (Editor), author. | Parr, Cynthia, author.
Identifiers: Canadiana 20190053461 | ISBN 9781988963051 (softcover)
Subjects: LCSH: Literature—Study and teaching (Higher)
Classification: LCC PN59 .H86 2019 | DDC 809.0071—dc23

CONTENTS

Acknowledgements	vii
Introduction	ix
Considerations for Developing an Introduction to Literature Course	3
Short Fiction	23
Non-Fiction	37
The Novel	49
Poetry	61
Drama	75
Film	87
Teaching Fundamentals of Academic Argument	97
Appendix 1 Self-Reflection Questionnaire	113
Appendix 2 Syllabus for an Academic Year	115
Appendix 3 Thematic Readings for a Syllabus	121
Works Cited	125

Acknowledgements

We would like to thank these former and future colleagues for sharing their teaching experiences:

Cristina Artenie (PhD and former Lecturer at Laval University).

Peter Babiak (Instructor, Georgian College).

Bruce Gilchrist (Professor of English, John Abbott College, CEGEP).

Jeremy Johnson (PhD candidate and TA, Western University).

Adam Sol (Poet and Professor). His contribution is an excerpt from *How a Poem Moves*, ECW 2019, used by permission.

Alanda Theriault (Instructor, Georgian College).

We would also like to thank Universitas Press for the interest, encouragement, and enthusiasm they have invested in this project, and UBC Press for promoting and distributing our book across Canada.

Introduction

During our combined years of teaching, we have heard many colleagues' opinions about teaching Introduction to Literature. While some of these comments have been positive, many have reflected surprise and disappointment with students and with teaching experiences. Frequent observations have included dismay at students' perceived under-preparation for academia, entitlement, arrogance, and disrespect. Instructors have also expressed frustration with needing to cram so much material into an introductory course and being unable to progress at their preferred paces. They have bemoaned the amount of marking, expectations for communication with students, and their lack of enthusiasm for reading selections. We too have experienced some of these disappointments and have, at times, expressed our frustration with teaching first-year students. Gradually, however, we have reframed our experiences by attempting to reconsider first-year studies from the students' points of view. Despite continuing frustration at times, we now think of teaching first-year English as an opportunity to build bridges between relatively inexperienced students and the world of literary exploration in an academic environment.

Thinking about first-year students as a distinct population within the demanding educational context of academic study allows us to consider some of their unique experiences and characteristics. As students entering university are frequently required to enrol in several introductory courses in various disciplines, they may be expected to familiarize themselves with a variety of textual structures and reading conventions simultaneously (Pawan and Honeyford 27). Students may be assigned extensive readings in traditional textbooks, readers, trade books, and journals that differ in format, organization, perspective, vocabulary, and expression of ideas, depending upon their disciplines (Pugh, Pawan, and Antommarchi 30-32; Shanahan and Shanahan 48). They may be expected to adopt the practices of experienced disciplinary readers whose approaches may be influenced by their epistemologies and training relevant to the "intellectual values of a discipline and the methods by which scholarship is created" (Shanahan and Shanahan 50). Experienced readers of English literature, for example, focusing on the importance of text and context, may emphasize close, analytical reading, construction of arguments, and perspectives of literary criticism in order to evaluate the validity of interpretations (Donald 242; Foster xiii). These are skills that are acquired in a first-year course and refined through time and practice.

Against a backdrop of rigorous expectations for students entering universities, students themselves may perceive university study differently than their professors. Newson characterized students as "'autonomous choosers' in the educational products market" who may enter university with a consumerist attitude that affects their perceptions of course selection and content, grading, and personal responsibility for attendance and studying (230). Students may be disengaged with their required courses and with classroom environments that encourage deep learning, resulting in alienation and stress (Côté and Allahar 93). Frequently, students may prioritize earning the credential, rather than deep learning, as their primary goal in university study (Roberts and Roberts 128-29).

An apparent preference for efficient earning of credentials and, frequently, surface learning may not be a matter of student choice exclusively, however. Tagg suggests that students may have adopted "global mindsets to academic tasks, to studying and school work" within contexts of formal education that encourage surface learning (82). Surface learning is characterized by static reception of "discrete bits of data" as well as a focus on tasks themselves, and it may provide an unpleasant experience (Tagg 81). Students who have not been encouraged to engage with active or deep learning may adopt a surface orientation to education that may continue throughout university study (Donald 12; Popovic and Green chap 2, par 2).

Clearly, not all students perceive university study negatively or are unprepared to participate effectively. Regardless of their goals and prior educational experiences, however, first-year university students may face particular challenges when transitioning from secondary to postsecondary education—a complex, unfamiliar academic environment in which they are expected to participate fully and immediately (Donald 11; Pugh et al. 26). Researchers have estimated that of the total "gains

Introduction

students make in knowledge and cognitive skill development" during university, more than two-thirds occurs during the first two years of study (Reason, Terenzini, and Domingo 149), thus positioning the early years of university as critical to "laying the foundation on which [students'] subsequent academic success and persistence rest" (150).

One of students' challenges is the need to meet rigorous academic standards, largely by reading and learning independently (Donald xi-xii; Pugh et al. 25, 39). Deep reading comprehension is required in order for students to navigate through reading assignments and to function as creative, critical thinkers (Mann 298; Pawan and Honeyford 26). From a cognitive perspective, first-year university students are encouraged to engage in forms of active reading, higher-order thinking, and critical response that satisfy criteria for engaged learning (Halpern 451; Mulcahy-Ernt and Caverly 181). However, students may experience difficulties meeting these criteria as the volume of reading, the diversity of topics, and the variety of assigned tasks may make significant demands on students' cognitive processing abilities (Taraban, Rynearson, and Kerr 283).

Although university students are often referred to as adult learners, most first-year students are completing adolescence and entering into young adulthood (Alexander and Fox 158). As such, their development as adults is just beginning and some of their physical and cognitive development is still emerging (Alexander and Fox 158). Alexander and Fox identified several developmental processes that occur in typical adolescents. These include biophysiological (puberty and brain development), cognitive (increased thought capacity, knowledge automaticity, and self-awareness), psychosocial (identity development, self and social development), and contextual changes (moves to unfamiliar school environments). Alexander and Fox associated these developmental processes with corresponding reading abilities and comprehension development in order to position adolescents as developing readers (170). For example, biophysiologically, as the density of grey and white matter in the brain changes, adolescents develop the ability to self-regulate and, therefore, may monitor their comprehension more effectively. Their "increased working memory capacity" may be "related to improved reading comprehension" (Alexander and Fox 159). Cognitively, adolescents may develop increased capacity for content knowledge, automaticity, and "strategic flexibility" that may be evident as "aspects of inferential and elaborative comprehension" develop during adolescence and beyond (Alexander and Fox 159). As late adolescents, traditional-aged first-year students may be described as developing readers in the sense that abilities necessary for effective university-level reading may still be emergent in their cognitive development.

In its positioning of lifelong reading development, Alexander's lifespan developmental perspective on reading provides a framework for discussion of students as travelers along a continuum of experience that ranges from acclimation to proficiency/expertise in terms of knowledge acquisition, interest, and strategic processing. Although students may enter university as proficient readers of familiar material, they may well find themselves in a state of acclimation when presented with the rigorous demands of university reading and discipline-specific texts (Alexander 415; Moje, Stockdill, Kim, and Kim 453). Readers in acclimation are likely to possess limited domain and topic knowledge, situational interest in reading, and surface-level strategic approaches to solve reading problems (Alexander 423-24). The model acknowledges that readers in acclimation, a vulnerable position, require "care and guidance" from those more familiar with "routines and rituals that are part of the domain culture" (Alexander 430), in this case professors, and that without this guidance, readers may struggle with comprehension and strategy use. Studies have found that as students' knowledge, interest, and strategic processing develop, their interaction with text becomes increasingly successful (Alexander 416).

In addition to cognitive and experiential factors affecting students' reading, sociopolitical and biographical realities are important to understanding what reading and writing mean to undergraduate students and consequently why they engage (or don't) in diverse ways (Mann 311). Reading for university courses becomes a public process, "evaluated through examinations, projects, essays, and seminar discussions" (Mann 312). Thus, previously private reading often turns public and is judged through tasks largely determined by others who hold positions of power (Mann 312). These judgments may affect the ways

Introduction

students see themselves in relation to the norms established by more experienced readers (Mann 313). When they believe that they are not succeeding, they may become threatened by the demands of academic reading and writing and avoid completing assignments (Mann 313). Over the years, we have become increasingly aware of the fear with which many first-year students approach university studies and have seen the effects of this fear on their ability to engage with tasks that we might consider foundational.

With these experiential, cognitive, sociopolitical, and biographical considerations in mind, attending to the particular challenges first-year students may face within the context of an Introduction to Literature course becomes important to an instructional approach. Students may or may not be aware of the effects of their prior education or of their current approaches to learning, but an instructor's awareness may inform reasonable expectations for student performance and influence course design. We are not suggesting that first-year instruction be watered down in any way, but rather that it be tempered with awareness of the thresholds across which many students must step as well as the importance of their instructors' encouragement and patience.

Our belief in developing a balanced approach to teaching Introduction to Literature – one in which rigorous standards are informed by realistic expectations – is one of the reasons we wanted to write this book. The potential within first-year students' threshold experiences is enormous. Yes, they may arrive with misconceptions about academic life and sometimes appear reluctant to engage fully with its work, but students also bring with them diverse backgrounds and experience, the enthusiasm and energy often associated with youth, and the ability, once challenged, to invest tremendous freshness and creativity in their studies. Once they are engaged, they can take responsibility for their learning and challenge themselves to enrich the depth and breadth of their understanding.

To that end, and with the hope that our teaching experiences will be useful for other instructors, we have included chapters on each of six genres frequently taught in an Introduction to Literature course. Each chapter includes teaching tips, hints for selecting readings, sample syllabi, ideas for in-class assignments and discussions, and writing assignments. None of the ideas included in the book is intended to be prescriptive: we offer a variety of readings and techniques that we have used over the years with no desire to present a packaged course. Instead, we hope that each chapter will inspire instructors (new, seasoned, and otherwise) to adapt the ideas that work for you and use them to enrich your personalized approaches to teaching. The genre chapters are bookended at the beginning with a discussion of considerations important to developing an introductory course, and at the end with a brief chapter on teaching writing fundamentals as well as appendices including questions for self-reflection, a sample syllabus for a full academic year, and ideas for cross-genre thematic connections.

Finally, we have developed our approaches to teaching Introduction to Literature in large part through conversations with one another (we shared an office for several years) and with our colleagues. We find this dialogue invaluable and would like to invite you to participate in dialogue with us and with one another. We hope you enjoy this book and look forward to hearing about your ideas for teaching Introduction to Literature!

Sylvia Hunt
Cynthia Parr
2018

Developing an Introduction to Literature Course

Considerations for Developing an Introduction to Literature Course

Departmental Contexts

Before planning an introductory course, it may be useful to learn about it from a departmental perspective. Asking other instructors, including the department chair, about the purpose of the course, expectations of student preparedness for continued studies in English, as well as other expectations (e.g., writing, study, and research skills) may provide a sense of the scope. Gathering anecdotal histories of teaching the course, including descriptions of successful instruction, may provide a sense of how the course fits into departmental culture. Asking for course descriptions and syllabi, if available, may provide a sense of both continuity and variation within delivery models for the course.

In our experience, the introductory course can be used as a catch-all for nearly everything first-year students may need to learn as they begin academic study. Expectations may include academic writing, study and research skills, literary vocabulary, analytical skills, as well as broad coverage of several literary genres and literary criticism. The scope and expectations for the course can easily become untenable, as a course in which too much material is presented in too little detail can be discouraging, frustrating, and overwhelming, and can damage interest in the course for both students and instructors. Asking specific questions initially may help in developing a syllabus that is challenging, but realistic. Questions to ask may include the following:

- Who are the students who normally take the course – all first-year? All English majors? Is the course mandatory for any students?
- How many students typically are in each class? Are there TAs assigned to the course?
- Does the course focus on literary genre? If not, what is its primary focus?
- To what extent does the course introduce students to researched writing, critical thinking, and response/journal forms of writing?
- Does the course include implicit instruction in academic reading and writing?
- Is the course considered remedial?
- Are there specific elements of the course agreed upon by the department?

While asking questions initially is important to course development, we also have found that ongoing discussion about the introductory course in an English department can keep it current and relevant, while allowing all instructors to maintain awareness of its various evolutions. Once the course is developed and taught the first time, it can be refined and adjusted. No syllabus is carved in stone; in fact, it should be adjusted regularly to reflect teaching and learning experiences.

Creating a Syllabus

It may be useful to take care of practical considerations early in the syllabus planning process. One consideration is the number of genres to be covered and the length of study for each. Dividing the semester into blocks may provide a reasonable framework upon which to build the course content. A course covering six genres across two semesters (short fiction, the novel, poetry, non-fiction, film, and drama), for example, will allow approximately four weeks for each, including in-class demonstrations of understanding. Remembering holidays and breaks, contingencies for cancelled classes, as well as high stress periods during which reading may be reduced, is important to a realistic allotment of time for each genre. Talking with students about their semesters as they unfold may provide candid revelations of peak study and learning times.

Another practical consideration is the progression of genres across the semesters of an academic year. Having a purpose for each placement, evident in a progression of ideas and emphases, will make sense to students and help them engage with course content. One way to order six genres is to approach short fiction, non-fiction, and the novel in the first semester, followed by poetry, drama, and film in the second semester (see Appendix 2). Making connections among the first three genres, then introducing the last three by drawing those connections forward, can give students a sense of continuity and purpose across the academic year of study.

Assigned Readings

Selecting readings for the course can be one of the most challenging aspects, especially when time is tight and expectations for content coverage are broad. One common approach is to use an anthology of literature for the course and draw readings from it. It is unusual, however, to find an anthology that fits the syllabus exactly, so some supplementation may be required. An important consideration for anthology selection is how much of the text will be used during class. Students may not view possession of an underused anthology as positively as instructors might; optics are important, as is consideration of students' financial investment in their textbooks. One alternative to a large anthology is several smaller texts containing the specific works that will be studied. Online versions of older works may be useful as well, supplemented by handouts adhering to the university's copyright agreements.

Selecting a theme for readings is one way to organize them (see Appendix 3). A theme such as feminist literatures can connect genres and provide threads for discussion and writing. A thematic approach can be open to each instructor's preferences or may support a university's teaching interests. Students may benefit from seeing organized paths through their exploration of each genre that may prevent them from feeling overwhelmed.

Introduction to Literature

One downside to thematic approaches is that students who do not engage personally with the chosen theme may find assigned readings challenging or even off-putting. They may learn to engage, but if they do not, there will be no respite for them in a variety of works on one theme.

Another method of selecting and organizing readings is to provide as much diversity as possible: deliberately choosing works that vary in terms of authors' ethnicity, gender, age, geographic location, and subject matter is one way to introduce students to a range of writing. Calling attention to the variety may help students to appreciate multiple voices and situations in literature and may provide an opportunity for many students to identify with at least one author who speaks to them. One downside to such variety is that it may lack organization and become overwhelming for some students. Hopping around through time periods, locations, cultures, etc. may be exciting and challenging for instructors and some students, but confusing for others.

Our priority in text selection is that works should be interesting for first-year students. Often that interest can be established through relevance to students' lives. Selecting protagonists who are close in age to traditional students, modern texts that reflect modern mores, non-fiction texts that discuss students' learning, and works that discuss current issues can all inspire students to participate in the active reading and critical analysis that are goals of an introductory course. Students who choose to major in English will take specific courses later in their studies (e.g., Renaissance Literature) in which they will work through the canon. Students in first-year courses do well to hone reading and analytical skills first, so they can apply them to more advanced study in all disciplines. This approach does not condone watering down any course material; rather, it prioritizes the student experience so that students may learn how to approach their studies actively and effectively.

Reaching a balance between high expectations and overload in terms of volume and difficulty of reading assignments is critical to students' compliance and engagement with texts. It may be useful to consider students' full cross-course reading loads and the challenges, particularly in first-year studies, of time management and completion of all readings and assignments for all courses. Developing a specific purpose for the inclusion of each text and considering each one in relation to the others may provide variety and maximize the reading experience associated with each text. Making individual texts count, rather than piling on the complete works of an author, for example, may be more useful at this stage of students' studies. We find that reviewing and rebalancing the assigned readings at the end of each academic year is a productive way to update course content.

Expressing clear expectations for how and why students are asked to read specific works – what they are looking for and how they may find it – may encourage students to complete assigned readings and provide topics for discussion in class. The more specific the reading instructions, and the more clearly the instructions are related to the syllabus, the better prepared students may be to participate, and the richer class discussions and activities will be. Incorporating reading instruction as an integral part of the course is addressed briefly below.

Writing Assignments

If you think back to your own experience in an Introduction to Literature course, you may have been asked to write traditional papers, perhaps one or two per semester. Panicking over these assignments may appear now simply part of paying the dues of becoming a scholar, but there are alternatives to traditional assignments that may be more effective. How practical is it to assign a lengthy paper for the first assignment when students most likely have had little preparation in academic writing of this type? Again, we stress the importance of understanding students' experience levels as well as departmental expectations around written assignments:

- What types of writing have students completed previously?
- Have their prior English courses prepared them for analytical writing?
- What are desired writing outcomes for the course – and are they best reached through frequent analysis of specific works or longer essays?
- Is emphasis placed on students exploring their own ideas in their writing or utilizing researched sources?

Working within departmental parameters, it may be possible to incorporate writing process assignments that allow students to focus on well-defined tasks while developing skills and confidence gradually. For example, across a semester, assignments may begin with in-class response, followed by critical response and analysis, and finally, a full essay, thus increasing levels of complexity with each assignment. Within a research essay assignment as well, components may be submitted and assessed to assist students with their writing processes: these components may include a proposed topic and thesis; an annotated bibliography; and/or an outline or draft. Allowing time for students to submit process assignments, receive assessment, and utilize each one in the preparation of the next can be challenging in a packed semester, but with careful planning, each assignment can contribute to a thread of increasingly challenging tasks that introduce students to a variety of university-level writing assignments. Details of process assignments for researched essays are discussed below.

An important consideration in planning a progression of readings and assignments is student attendance. While most students may attend regularly, some will miss classes and want to 'make up' the work. In a finely-tuned syllabus in which every class counts, this can be challenging, as students may have missed the instruction around assignments, as well as discussion of class content to inform their writing. Thinking through a contingency plan for these students may be useful. There are no easy answers here – we still struggle with how to deal with these situations fairly – but before students ask, it may be useful to speak with other instructors about policies at your university and to clarify your own boundaries.

Incorporating Reading, Writing, and Research Skills Instruction

University students are often expected to read actively in order to learn, write well in a variety of formats, and research effectively. If first-year students have not been prepared to engage with these processes prior to their introductory courses, they soon discover the need to develop these abilities as quickly as possible. Some students acquire skills independently over time, others may take advantage of support services, but all students may benefit from guidance as they learn to function effectively in a rigorous academic environment; an introductory course may provide some of that important guidance. While the primary purpose of Introduction to Literature may not be to introduce students to academic reading, writing, and research skills, there are ways to incorporate some guidance for students as they study literary genres.

Reading

Reading processes are often taken for granted, particularly by instructors who may be successful readers themselves. However, it is not unusual for students to be unsure of how to approach reading assignments: our first-year students have reported spending hours reading and not comprehending the material, or spending little time reading and therefore being unprepared for class discussions. Extensive instruction in comprehension may not be realistic in this situation, but a few tips may be offered. For example, calling attention to the importance of active reading as preparation for class, specifically by providing reading goals and tasks, may help students to become familiar with reading to learn and analyze (processes with which they may be less familiar than reading to memorize).

Sharing your own reading processes (particularly those learned early in your career), as well as tips from other sources, can provide concrete help for students who may deal with fear of approaching extensive readings, not just in English but across the several disciplines of their introductory courses. Reading tips do not need to be discussed in great detail; they can be incorporated as part of introductory comments on reading assignments. Questions to consider may include these:

- How should students read the first time through a text – just for enjoyment, or with specific tasks in mind?
- How can students break up assigned texts in order to comprehend them?

- What should students do if they do not understand a text? (re-reading rarely helps)
- What do you expect students to know about the text by the time they attend class?

We have found that, while some students will resist preparing assigned readings for class discussion, with encouragement and guidance, most students will attempt to read prior to class, particularly if they can appreciate concrete advantages of doing so. Ongoing discussion about reading processes can be valuable.

Assuming that most students will arrive at class with assigned readings completed, another consideration is how to encourage them to utilize their understanding of the texts during lecture and/or discussion. One approach is to provide prepared questions. Distributing these questions at the beginning of class may encourage students to note their immediate responses and to take further notes during class to use later in written assignments. The questions and notes may jumpstart students' thinking processes about texts and inspire confidence in students who are not comfortable with extemporaneous response during class discussions.

Asking students to respond to interpretive questions (rather than factual ones) may set the tone for interactive discussion and encourage participation. The instructor's response to each student will also set the tone for discussion:

- Will students be ridiculed for expressing certain ideas (e.g., creationism)?
- Will their ideas be "shot down" if they are not consistent with the instructor's?
- How will expressions of racism, gender discrimination, etc. be handled during discussion?

While all potentialities cannot be foreseen, consideration of some of these scenarios prior to the first discussion may help instructors to promote respectful exchange and learning.

Consideration of others' voices is an important component of a first-year course, not only in discussion, but in reading and writing as well. As some students may have less diverse backgrounds than others and may not be accustomed to rigorous exchange of challenging ideas, providing guidelines for attending to others' voices may be useful. One such guideline can be a reminder that active reading involves not only developing a sense of personal response, but also a sense of appreciation for others' responses. This may seem obvious, but an introductory course may be the first space in which some students experience diversity of voices. Assuring them that considering a range of perspectives can strengthen, rather than threaten, their own voices may be useful.

Developing appreciation, not only for diversity, but for expertise as well, may be another beneficial goal for first-year students. Becoming aware of the range of voices in literary discussion, including those of seasoned thinkers, may be an unfamiliar experience for many students. Learning to appreciate wisdom gleaned from exposure to diverse voices, multiple genres, historical periods, cultural contexts, etc., can be pointed out as an important part of study in all academic disciplines. This is not to say, however, that students should strive to accept experts' ideas without analysis; critical reading is essential but becoming familiar with experienced voices within disciplines may be a first step toward establishing a foundation for informed critical analysis.

As students broaden their awareness through academic reading, discussion, and writing, their development of literary vocabulary may be a priority. If so, calling attention to terminology used during discussions, reviewing vocabulary as it is drawn from each genre to the next, and challenging students to use the vocabulary in their own work may encourage and reinforce learning without providing lists for memorization. Use of verbal cues to draw vocabulary, as well as other threads, through the course is one way of pointing out the framing of the course, and it may help students to stay organized and on track.

Writing

Specificity in writing assignments is important to first-year students who may not have written academic papers prior to their arrival. Clear, uncluttered instructions, preferably outlining steps to completion of assignments, may be very useful to all students including those of differing abilities and language experiences, non-traditional students, those who attend irregularly, etc. "Write a paper" may not be as useful an introduction to an assignment as outlining the steps involved in the process, particularly for the first assignment.

Many professors provide process assignments for researched essays so that students work through preparation in steps that are evaluated. Receiving feedback on these steps (and thus building their grade incrementally) may be much more useful to first-year students than receiving a single letter grade on a completed paper. Having said that, scheduling and grading multiple process assignments can become overwhelming for instructors. Keeping in mind the time involved, balanced against the potential advantage for students, may help to produce a reasonable number of assignments that allows students to receive invaluable feedback without overburdening the instructor. Reaching this reasonable number of assignments takes time and ongoing assessment of the goals and outcomes of each assignment.

There are many ways to approach process assignments: the purpose is to communicate with students before they attempt to write a finished product. For example, relevant to a paper's conceptualization, it may be necessary to teach the idea of a thesis statement in the context of academic argument. Asking students to submit a topic, a thesis idea – their stance for the paper – and a list of sources that they'll use in their argument may help students to organize their thoughts, even as you acknowledge that their stance may change as they write. We have found that conferences with students are extremely effective, both for students writing and instructors grading papers later. Making time for these conferences, however, can be challenging. Another way to check on students' planning processes for their papers is to require written submission of the elements mentioned above. While it takes longer to grade these submissions than it would to discuss them, scheduling for grading may be more feasible than scheduling conferences.

Convincing students to write a full draft, particularly early in the year, may be difficult if they are not accustomed to editing their writing. An alternative is to ask students to map their initial thinking in some way: some instructors prefer formal mind mapping, while others accept lists or diagrams – whatever helps students to think through and show their thesis, argument construction, and support before they begin writing. Another possibility is outlining an argument, although as many students are not familiar with this process, teaching it may take too much time. Working through a process of planning ideas, whatever your preference, may help students to formulate drafts of their writing that will be useful for your commentary and for their craftsmanship.

Requiring submission of process assignments establishes the idea of dialogue between students and the instructor. Submission to peers may also be considered, especially if students select the people with whom they wish to work. However, peer evaluation can easily be fruitless busy work unless students are guided in providing meaningful feedback (not just, "omg, I really liked this!"). Teaching respectful interactive response and monitoring those responses may be beyond the scope of the instructor's energy for this course; sometimes it makes more sense to plan a direct route through assignments, particularly in the first or second teaching of the course.

Our priorities for writing assignments include, as mentioned above, clear instructions that provide steps required for completion. These steps may seem obvious to instructors, but to first-year students with little academic writing experience, a thoughtfully laid-out work plan may be very helpful. Providing suggested topics for assignments is also useful for first-year students: often, they have not learned to conceptualize a project and plan its execution, so interesting topics may provide an important starting point. Even topics for journal responses can inspire students to engage with their writing. Without this focus, typical responses may include phrases such as, "I hated this book," followed by little explanation. Finally, another priority for us is to reach balance between structure and creative freedom: students need guidance, but they should also be responsible for their own thought processes and preparation of assignments. Providing too much information and too much help may discourage students from developing scholarly independence. This caveat can be applied to teaching, providing comments on assignments, and offering support during office hours and in emails.

Research

The art of research is not going to be perfected during an Introduction to Literature course but introducing important features of research processes is certainly possible. Talking about the existence and purpose of documentation styles early in the course (preferably on the first day) will establish the importance of MLA to writing and reading about literature in an academic environment. Mentioning documentation frequently during discussions of writing and reading may help students to see and appreciate its integration in the discipline and help them to understand the university's and your emphases on adhering to its principles. Additionally, integrating completion of a library research skills module within the grades for the course may prove beneficial for students and for you as an instructor with limited teaching time. The university library may offer a certificate that students can earn outside of class time. Content may include approaches to research, location of materials, search techniques, and documentation of sources. We have found that ongoing, respectful communication with librarians can enrich greatly the value of an Introduction to Literature course and can provide consistency across campus that students appreciate. Librarians who are aware of course content including assignments can provide invaluable support for first-year students who may struggle with initiating research processes.

Assessment

Volumes have been written on methods of assessment, and we do not wish to duplicate or comment on that work here; instead, we offer the following points for consideration specific to our experiences with the development of an Introduction to Literature course.

The imbalance of power in a first-year classroom can be particularly evident in assessment. All instructors have the power to pass or fail students, but in first year, grades and comments may be perceived to carry particular weight. Students may be inexperienced academically and fearful of having their words and actions evaluated. They may have difficulty interpreting comments and grades. Simultaneously, some students may not demonstrate respect for instructors in ways that they may have decades ago and may look for streamlined ways to earn the marks they desire in their courses. Instructors, on the other hand, may use grades for several purposes: to reward complicit behavior, to 'weed out' those students they feel are unsuitable for academic pursuits, and/ or to strengthen their own teaching evaluations. Students who prioritize grades over learning and instructors who prioritize their own agendas may contribute tension to the inherent challenges of assessment processes.

While acknowledging that such challenges exist, we try to prioritize purpose in our design of assessment processes. Asking difficult questions about each assignment may help to establish appropriate assessment:

- What do I want students to demonstrate by completing this assignment?
- Are these demonstrations reasonable, considering the course and students' prior experience?
- Which specific elements will I be looking for, and how do I want students to incorporate them?
- How will I communicate with students my perceptions of their understanding while encouraging them to evaluate their own learning?

Focusing on a limited number of priorities when marking an assignment may help students to focus their craftsmanship and editing. While it may require great self-control not to fix every spelling or grammar error, establishing marking priorities may reduce stress and provide focus for both students and instructors. In the first assignment, for example, if two priorities such as sentence structure and word usage are established, in the second assignment those elements plus two more may become the priorities. Communication of these priorities for each assignment is critical.

Communicating with students about the use of comments in grading can also be very helpful. Students who focus on grades alone may not read comments initially but providing an explanation of why and how you comment may encourage them to engage with assessment more fully. Focusing on the stated goals of an assignment and using clear, concise, consistent language may strengthen content of comments, as may keeping in mind the audience and students' likely unfamiliarity with the need to read, interpret, and respond to the comments. Talking about this before returning the first assignment may be useful.

Taking the time to prepare an assessment approach may be a worthwhile investment for both instructors and students. Focusing on purpose and priorities in assessment may help instructors to draw parameters around an element of teaching that can consume excessive time and energy if not controlled in some way. Respectful clarity and specificity in assignment instructions, marking schemes, comments, and in-class explanations may help students learn course content and monitor their learning as well.

Quizzes

For some information (e.g., plot details, documentation format, plagiarism), using short quizzes may help to confirm whether or not students have understood the basics. Paper quizzes can be time consuming in their preparation and marking; however, online programs like Kahoot!, a quiz-generating program/platform, are very useful for ascertaining students' understanding. Kahoot! is free, many students may have used it in high school, and instructors are given immediate feedback if something is not understood.

Students' success with these quizzes may be included in your marking scheme. Some students are reluctant to contribute to class discussion; if you give any marks for participation, these students are immediately punished for their reticence. If they demonstrate their knowledge in these quizzes, however, some marks can be given for this.

Use of Media

A variety of media can be incorporated in an Introduction to Literature course, not only because students may be comfortable with this approach but because of the depth and richness of materials available. Students may benefit from hearing recordings of readings, considering visual images that portray topics of literary works, exploring topical controversies through film and music, etc. The days of tacking on a video to keep students' interest during class (a suspect practice at best!) are long gone: it now makes sense to integrate the most effective means of communicating ideas and to layer a variety of approaches to augment consideration of the written word. Challenging students to sharpen their perceptions and receptions of ideas presented in literature contextually is an important goal for an introductory course, as it may contribute to a foundation for broad critical response and analysis.

Some instructors may be familiar with multi-media sources relevant to discussions of literature and may take their inclusion for granted, while others may embrace the notion less whole heartedly. Students may be well versed in use of social media but be less familiar with learning that draws on a variety of works inspired by ideas represented in literature. Much learning can occur through selection and critique of multi-media as well as through exploration of its content. Instructors can take advantage of the many resources now available to assist with developing this approach, while students may also be able to add ideas for media to the course. We support an integrated approach to purposeful learning and encourage dialogue with students about contexts relevant to the literature studied.

First Class and Last Class

Especially with a course as broad reaching as this one, it can be difficult for students to appraise their learning and draw from it as they move forward in their studies. Some students may be anxious simply to complete the course and move on to the 'real' content of their degrees, while others may struggle to the end with the most basic demands of introductory course content. Articulating clear goals for the course at the beginning, reminding students of progress made in satisfying those goals, and then asking them to engage in review and assessment of the course at the end can provide and maintain some shape and purpose for the course.

After providing a clear overview during the first class, it may be useful to ask students to write about their responses to the information. Encouraging students to be honest, to ask questions, and to disclose any information they would like you to have about them may lay a foundation for ongoing individual dialogue (all information should, of course, be kept confidential). Keeping these responses and returning them to students during the last class can be an effective way for students to evaluate their own growth and to provide an instructor with insight into their perceptions of the course. Looking at their initial responses and then considering their progress may also help students to think of a course as a progression of ideas and their learning within it as a journey to be continued in future studies.

There are many ways to utilize the first class to set course parameters and the last class to contextualize learning and celebrate achievement. For example, during the first class, asking students to read a short piece, formulate a response, and discuss it in small groups before bringing ideas to a class discussion, may set the tone for future discussions of assigned readings and demonstrate the importance of completing those readings before each class. Maximizing the opportunity to welcome students to the learning environment and to communicate expectations while they are open minded and enthusiastic can (and should) involve much more than simply reading the syllabus.

The last class of a semester before final exams can be celebratory. Reviewing the content covered within the contexts of course goals and intentional progression of ideas may help students to appreciate their learning as well as to prepare for the exam. Calling attention to achievements is important, as is setting goals for further study, and this can be accomplished in a variety of ways that suit both the instructor's and students' styles. The point is not to let the course fizzle out at the end but rather to cap it with acknowledgement of processes and achievements associated with academic learning.

Bottom Lines

There is a difference between streamlining an approach to an Introduction to Literature course and dumbing down the material. Practical considerations are important when developing any course, and they certainly are in an introductory course. Instructors may need to deal with diverse, inexperienced students in short blocks of class time, possibly within contexts of high departmental expectations, even as they are cognizant of a need to preserve personal wellbeing while balancing the daily demands of course delivery and marking. We learned over time to select topics and readings carefully, and then to pack their presentation with rich and important elements relevant and interesting to a variety of students.

It is important to establish an environment designed for success contingent upon students investing effort and hard work in their studies. Such an environment can be developed and maintained through clear communication, reasonable expectations, and accessible support. Simultaneously, it is important to seek balance between offering students a rich introductory experience and maintaining instructor energy through monitoring types of evaluation, hours required for preparation of each unit, etc. Both students and the instructor should enjoy the course and learn from its presentation.

It takes time to develop an approach to an introductory course that works for both students and the instructor. Asking students for feedback regularly, maintaining dialogue with other instructors, and conducting an informal review each year can help to keep the course relevant and fresh and make it enjoyable for both students and the instructor.

Short Fiction

Short Fiction

When teaching an Introduction to Literature course, short fiction can be a good place to start. Most of the vocabulary (character, setting, point-of-view, theme) that will be used and applied to the other, more complex genres is introduced here in connection with shorter texts. This limited length can also be less daunting than a novel for first-year students. This is not to imply that short stories are simple in their construction; in fact, they are deceptively complex. However, in a study by Charles Duke, students tended to find the short story one of the most satisfying forms to begin their literary analysis (62). In addition, some instructors agree that short stories often provide more challenge and hold students' interest better initially than works from other genres:

- Their brevity makes them ideal for class discussion.
- Readers of various abilities have little difficulty reading and finishing short stories.
- Short stories allow students in an introductory course to explore specific elements of fiction in depth.

Teaching Tips

The standard elements of fiction to teach are

- Plot
- Character
- Setting
- Point-of-view or narrative voice
- Symbol
- Theme

These six elements are common to all genres that are generally taught in an Introduction to Literature course since these are the means by which a story is told. It is the way in which each genre uses these elements that is of importance. Medium – stage, screen, page – also has an effect on how each of these elements is to be interpreted.

Choosing Reading Selections

1. Most anthologies include a wide variety of short fiction; sometimes this enormous offering can make it difficult to select a few stories that fit nicely into the limited time allotted in the syllabus for the genre. Added to this is the conundrum of what 'must' be taught. Looking through the long list of stories in an anthology, we read the titles of well-known pieces by Faulkner, Lawrence, O'Connor and Updike (to name a few). In that list are also lesser-known selections, possibly ones we have never read ourselves. This creates a challenge – do we teach stories that we feel students should know because they are considered canonical (and possibly within our own comfort zones) or do we include more experimental or non-traditional readings? Often, instructors get caught up in the "but they *must* read this one" approach, forgetting that many canonical texts will probably be covered in other courses for English majors. In fact, newer fiction might be more challenging and interesting to students since stories like "The Lottery" or "A Rose for Emily" may have already been covered in high school.

2. In addition to the typical short story, consider including short-short stories or micro-fiction. This is a sub-genre of short fiction that consists of stories less than 1,500 words long. This type of short story gained attention with the invention and use of Twitter and with authors like David Mitchell experimenting with the possibilities and limitations of the electronic medium for storytelling. Including this type of short fiction, contrasted with the more conventional short story, encourages students to consider what 'story' is. With micro-fiction, the reader becomes more involved in the story

process, having to create sense out of limited information. Here are just a few examples of micro-fiction:

> a. "Love and Other Catastrophes: A Mix Tape" by Amanda Brown is a story which consists only of song titles that describe the development of a romantic relationship. Students might initially question how this can be considered a story since it visually defies expectations.
>
> b. "Slide to Unlock" by Ed Park is a stream-of-consciousness meditation on passwords and how those numbers are a form of autobiography (ending with a dark twist).
>
> c. "Discovering America" by Stephen Graham Jones is an exploration of both aboriginality and imposed identity.
>
> d. "Sticks" by George Saunders describes loss and family relationships.

Teaching Tips

1. When selecting stories, keep in mind how some of them may be included in discussion in later genre sections. For example, some stories have been made into films available for viewing on YouTube. "Sticks," "Gryphon," "The Yellow Wallpaper" and "The Lottery" are only a few stories that have been made into films. Consider how the story changes when transposed to a different medium.

2. Look at short fiction that is considered 'canonical' (fits the standard form of what we consider to be a story). Then, challenge these assumptions about what a story 'is' with really modern ideas about the short story (blogged short fiction, stories like "Love and Other Catastrophes: A Mix Tape"). How do these stories challenge what we believe to be a story?

3. Contexts for interpretation: Viewing short fiction through a literal or technical lens or frame, a historical lens or frame, or a critical lens or frame can help us to understand it more fully and provide alternative perspectives.

> a. Literary terminology will develop as various perspectives are considered and interpretations are explored – quick quizzes on terminology presented to date with no grading may help students to gauge their own comprehension and discuss terminology with others (self-graded and compared).

4. Consider incorporating an essay about fiction in the section. Genres are not written in isolation: fiction authors write about their craft just as researchers write about students (students may find it a surprise that they are the subject of research). Reading what an author has to say about fiction and the importance of reading fiction helps to contextualize the genre. Here are a few examples of essays that work well in the discussion about fiction:

> a. Why our Future Depends on Libraries, Reading and Daydreaming" by Neil Gaiman
>
> b. "Truth" from *Why Read* by Mark Edmundson
>
> c. "Preface" from *The Triumph of Narrative* by Robert Fulford

Syllabus Ideas

Each academic institution has its own format for class length (e.g., 60 minutes, 90 minutes, three hours). We will use three hours as the basis of our syllabus examples and content. Having a clear idea about what will be done and how long it will take is essential if material is to be covered in those limited class periods.

There is no correct way to organize a syllabus as it is a very personal reflection of our own teaching interests. The following examples are simply ideas for creating a syllabus and some of the considerations or methods that can go into its organization.

Sample 1 – This example is based on teaching the elements of fiction.

	Topic	Readings
Week 1	**Character-based stories** – some stories are all about exploring character. Round vs flat; realistic vs caricature; likeable vs disagreeable	"Miss Brill" by Katherine Mansfield "Gryphon" by Charles Baxter "Story of an Hour" by Kate Chopin
Week 2	**Setting-based stories** – some stories explore setting and how it affects plot or character History – understanding the time-period is essential Geography – language, customs, landscape, urban or rural	"Everyday Use" by Alice Walker "New York Day Women" by Edwidge Danticat "The Yellow Wallpaper" by Charlotte Perkins Gilman
Week 3	**Point-of-view stories** First-person, third-person, reliable, unreliable	"The Cask of Amontillado" by Edgar Allan Poe "The Lottery" by Shirley Jackson
Week 4	**Symbol and theme** Use of symbols Theme – what the author wants us to know beyond the plot.	"Doe Season" by David Michael Kaplan "A Worn Path" by Eudora Welty

Sample 2 - This example looks at canonical fiction alongside more experimental stories and alternative authorial voices.

	Topic	Readings
Week 1	Famous short stories Why are they so important?	"The Cask of Amontillado" by Edgar Allan Poe "Young Goodman Brown" by Nathaniel Hawthorne "A Rose for Emily" by William Faulkner
Week 2	Post-colonial voices – alternative voices and stories	"Discovering America" by Stephen Graham Jones "Borders" by Thomas King "This is What it Means to Say Phoenix, Arizona" by Sherman Alexie "New York Day Women" by Edwidge Danticat
Week 3	Alternative forms – micro-fiction	"Slide to Unlock" by Ed Park "Sticks" by Karl Edward Wagner "Love and Other Catastrophes: A Mix Tape" by Amanda Brown
Week 4	Graphic fiction – images and dialogue, reading 'cells,' comics vs graphic novels	"Persepolis" by Marjane Satrapi

Short Fiction

Sample 3 - A third example introduces students to a theoretical perspective or lens by which stories are written or interpreted.

In this case, feminist criticism is the frame for story selection.

	Topic	**Readings**
Week 1	The tormented female narrator	"Story of an Hour" by Kate Chopin "The Yellow Wallpaper" by Charlotte Perkins Gilman
Week 2	Girls and boys	"Boys and Girls" by Alice Munro "Unpopular Gals" by Margaret Atwood
Week 3	Male voice, female experience, myth reinvented	"Rappaccini's Daughter" (contrast with Midas myth) by Nathaniel Hawthorne "The Birthmark" by Nathaniel Hawthorne
Week 4	Mothers and their children	"I Stand Here Ironing" by Tillie Olsen "A Story for Children" by Svava Jakobsdottir

Getting Started

When introducing a new genre, consider conducting a Self-Reflection Questionnaire, asking students to think about their prior experiences with and feelings about the genre (see Appendix 1 for example). Ask students to keep this questionnaire in their portfolios (see Writing Assignments below) for reconsideration when the unit is completed; being able to read their initial thoughts once they have studied a genre may help students to gain perspective on their learning. You may also wish to conduct a Post-Study Questionnaire at the end of each genre to provide an opportunity for students to reflect on their new (or unchanged) perspectives (see Appendix 1).

> Literature is other people. Not just 'about' other people, it is other people. Every text comes to us from the past, calling with a voice, the voice of a person who is asking to be read, to be heard in the future. To read attentively is therefore to bring that person to life again, to step back in time to another place, another world, another person's being; it's not about you. Literature, or rather fiction, be it a novel, a poem, a play, a painting, or a film, is thus the best empathy machine there is: it works across boundaries of space and time to make you feel and think as someone else did who isn't you, and that confers great responsibility to hear that person, to try to think like her. Learning something about yourself is the side benefit.
>
> Bruce Gilchrist

Once students have completed their individual questionnaires, initiate a general discussion about what they expect from the genre, in this case short fiction:

- What preconceived notions do they have about the genre?
- Do any of them read short fiction? If they do, why do they like it? If they don't, why not?
- Why would a writer prefer this form over the longer novel form?
- What are the limits of short fiction?

- We often associate short fiction with children's fiction and the longer novel with more mature readership – why does length seem to have a bearing on reader maturity?

In order to provide some context for the class, a short lecture is often useful. For example, if 'character' is the discussion point for the class, provide information on what is meant by character types or character-driven stories. Ask for examples students might have encountered in other stories, TV shows or films. Then proceed to a short assignment you may have prepared to get students thinking about the material (see below for some ideas). In other classes, forgo the short assignment for an in-class written project. Finally, have students engage in discussion about the stories that were read for class. We have found that prepared discussion questions help direct focus and conversation.

Gaining student engagement can be difficult initially; students are new to the classroom, to each other, to you, and, possibly, to the notion that their input is essential to the learning process. In order to gain their engagement and ownership of their personal class preparation and participation, it may be useful to ask for a quick synopsis of character, plot, etc. at the beginning of each class. This allows most students to capture the gist of the piece of short fiction and may increase engagement. It may also encourage students inspired by, rather than excluded from, a discussion to complete the reading after class (completion is, after all, the point!); some students, however, may wait for the synopsis in class to get the gist of the short story, rather than reading at home first. Assigning points toward the participation mark in the course for accurate synopses may provide some motivation. Synopsis does not need to take very long, and in fact, positioning it as a quick first step to discussion of a work may demonstrate to students that there is so much more to glean from a short story.

In-Class Assignments and Discussion Ideas

These simple ideas can be either discussion-based activities or short written assignments done in class.

1. Formulating a one-sentence plot synopsis can be an effective tool for both story comprehension and writing skills. Most plot-summaries are a 'blow-by-blow' account of the plot. Once students wrestle with the one-sentence limit, they will come to terms with the central action or theme of the story.

2. Characterization is essential to a good story. Students often forget that relatability is not important to understanding fiction; they do not have to like or relate to a character. However, they must attempt to understand that character and his/her motivation. As a simple exercise, provide students with a scenario and ask them to describe the character and his/her actions. For example, you could provide the following information:

   a. A young man finds a wallet on the street.

      i. What if it is in a 'nice' neighborhood? What might we expect from the character?

      ii. If it is on a busy street of a large city?

      iii. If the young man is very poor? What might it imply about character if he attempts to return the wallet?

      iv. What if the character who finds the wallet is an older woman? What might we expect from such a character? What would be our reaction if she does not do as expected?

      v. What conflicts (both internal and external) might arise in this situation?

   b. Encourage students to explore expectations they may have about character, gender, setting, and conflict. How does an author defy those expectations?

   c. Film and print media often rely on visual images to create an indication of character. Clothing, hair color, and facial expression all give immediate impressions. However, authors of short stories often supply the reader with little information about a character; it is left to the reader to make judgments. Create a few PowerPoint slides of various people and ask students how they rely on visual clues to determine character. What do their facial expressions imply about character? What are they wearing and what does that mean? How does 'reading' an image correspond to reading text to obtain information about a character? Can that reading be mistaken? Can immediate assumptions about a characteristic lead us to false impressions (e.g., a fur coat immediately means wealth)?

3. Stock characters have a long history in fiction and drama. Ask students what common characters are found in fiction, television shows, and movies. What role does the 'stock character' have in storytelling?

4. Legend has it that Hemingway's favorite piece of his own writing was a six-word short story: "For sale: baby shoes, never worn."

>a. What is the 'story' behind the story? How can these six words be considered a story? What does the reader 'bring' to this sentence in order to create a story?

>b. Normally we immediately read a tale of personal tragedy. Can we imagine a story that is not tragic?

>c. How does this sentence both conform to and defy the definition of 'story'?

Writing Assignments

As stated in the Considerations chapter, writing in a first-year course may be much more process-oriented than in upper years of study; students must come to terms with what is expected with respect to accountability for their ideas, critical analysis, development of argument, etc.

Here are a few suggestions:

1. Have students keep a writing portfolio. Ask them to purchase a binder in which all their writing assignments and assessments can be kept. At the time of submission, the binder with all its contents is handed in. This allows you to look at each student's progression in writing and critical thinking. Students can also keep track of their progress as they work through the course. A meeting with each student about progress midway through the course helps to emphasize student learning and indicate where work might still be needed.

2. For each genre, have students write a focused journal response. This is not a 1st-person assessment of a specific story, stating why or why not it was liked. Instead, it should be a focused response and critical analysis. It is a good idea to provide specific questions upon which a response can be prepared, as first-year students are often not prepared to come up with suitably complex questions.

3. Do in-class short writing assignments. Again, these should be based around focused questions. These will encourage reading prior to class, as students will not wish to be caught with nothing to say. Answers to these questions may be shared within a small group or the whole class as a basis for discussion of specific stories.

Non-Fiction

Non-Fiction

Non-fiction can be one of the most challenging sections in a genre course to teach. It is not that it is a difficult genre; as academics, we understand this form since it is the basis of our professional communication. In the classroom, in the office, at our conferences, in our research, we communicate through academic prose. We are experts at it; we enjoy reading and writing it. Teaching it to non-experts, however, can be the problem.

In general, the other literary genres normally taught in a first-year course are easily identifiable and familiar to students. Most will have encountered fiction, plays and poetry in their previous education. These works fit easily into a category and students have little difficulty identifying them. Non-fiction, however, can be more difficult. First, it is such an enormous category: biographies, autobiographies, history, diaries, academic papers, journalism, literary criticism are only a few of the many types of non-fiction. For an instructor, it can sometimes be difficult to know where to start. Another common difficulty has more to do with the perception of the genre. Students often associate non-fiction/fact with uninteresting. Poetry may be thought 'difficult' and plays 'confusing,' but the death-knell to student engagement is 'boring.'

It may be tempting to omit non-fiction from the course since it is so less easily defined than the other genres. However, it does contain definite cross-overs with other genres as well as introduce students to the basics of rhetoric that will be useful in other courses. According to Charles Bazerman, non-fiction "helps us see the purposefulness and flexibility of form, rather than form being just a matter of correctness and fulfillment of a few school-based tasks, created purely for instruction and assessment" (xi). As with the fiction genres, non-fiction allows for a specific presentation of or engagement with emotions, pleasures, or social and personal issues. Despite its challenges, non-fiction may enrich literary study and open doors for students to the complexities (and pleasures) of well-constructed argument.

Teaching Tips

1. One of the more engaging forms to teach is literary (also known as creative) non-fiction. In general, literary non-fiction is a diverse genre; written in prose, it can tread a fine line between fiction and academic non-fiction. Writers of literary non-fiction often incorporate elements of fiction into their prose: symbols, character development, setting, etc. (elements that also will be seen in the other genres). Unlike the impersonal academic essay which relies solely on facts to prove its hypothesis, literary non-fiction also elicits an emotional response from the reader.

2. The term 'essay' is used both in academic writing and literary non-fiction, and this can be confusing for students. Particularly if you teach short fiction first and introduce an essay on the genre in that context, in this section it will be important to clarify and define the term 'literary non-fiction'. We learned the importance of this distinction in one of our classes: after teaching literary non-fiction and then asking students to write an 'essay' on a topic about the genre, we ended up with a stack of creative non-fiction instead of the academic analysis expected. For this reason, it may be useful to differentiate clearly between literary non-fiction as a work in prose that uses literary devices to argue a stance, and academic writing as a work in prose that uses academic sources and recognizable formatting to develop an argument. By avoiding the term 'essay' (a vague word that covers many types of non-fiction writing), students will have a clearer idea of what to expect in both their reading and writing.

Choosing Reading Selections

Let's start with some of the challenges of selecting material for this section:

1. Some anthologies do not include a section of non-fiction in their contents. This omission can be both positive and negative. On one hand, instructors are left to find their own readings. This raises the question of where to begin in that search. With so much to choose from, it can be hard to make a choice. Then comes the issue of making copies available to students, either in paper form or online, without encountering copyright issues. On the other hand, not being limited to what an anthology has to offer means that you are free to pick whatever you feel most passionate about. An instructor's enthusiasm for material is often contagious.

2. Whether an anthology includes non-fiction, or you select readings yourself, be aware that there may be an enormous gap between your knowledge of the genre and content and the students' familiarity. Sometimes this information gap will affect student engagement with a reading, particularly with non-fiction which assumes a certain level of knowledge in the reader. For example, Jonathan Swift's satirical essay "A Modest Proposal" is a classic in the genre of non-fiction. However, before some students are able to grasp Swift's intentions, they need to be given an overview of Irish history in the 18th century. On one occasion, we thought of using John McPhee's very creative essay "The Search for Marvin Gardens" which compares the game *Monopoly* with the urban squalor of Atlantic City. The fact that almost one half of the class had never played the game *Monopoly* posed a serious problem in understanding McPhee's argument.

3. We have also found that using academic papers as a comparison to literary non-fiction can be overwhelming for first-year students. The specific language or technical jargon associated with whatever field a paper addresses, as well as the complexities of format, are appreciated most fully with experience. Introducing first-year students to analytical academic writing is critical at this stage, but in-depth analysis of an academic paper is often not possible at the first-year level.

Teaching Tips

With these considerations in mind, and using our focus on literary non-fiction, here are some suggestions for the selection process:

1. Consider selecting readings that discuss a similar topic or issue. Presenting multiple stances on a topic can introduce the idea of rigorous, controlled argument and help students to engage with viewpoints different from their own (see Syllabus Ideas, Sample 1).

2. Selection of types of works may be influenced by the purpose of including non-fiction readings in the course: is there, for example, a departmental emphasis on history or literary criticism? If so, examples of literary non-fiction should address these areas, perhaps without delving into great complexity at this point. Arguments that define terminology and broad concepts, for example, may provide useful background and introduction to a field such as literary criticism. A series of works written by authors across a specified timespan may complement an historical departmental emphasis (see Syllabus Ideas, Sample 2).

3. Consider drawing literary devices forward from the short fiction section by pairing works of literary non-fiction with stories already discussed. This may be done in terms of symbols, points of view, setting, etc. that may be utilized in works from both genres. Discussion of these cross-genre pairings will depend upon the way your syllabus is developed, so we have provided examples of literary non-fiction only that emphasize literary device (see Syllabus Ideas, Sample 3).

Non-Fiction

Syllabus Ideas

Sample 1– This example is theme-based, each week presenting a selection of readings on a specific theme but presenting different views.

	Topic	Readings
Week 1	Racism	"I Have a Dream" by Martin Luther King Jr. "Pretty Like a White Boy" by Drew Hayden Taylor "I'm Not Racist But…" by Neil Bissoondath
Week 2	Students and Academia	"Taking Women Students Seriously" by Adrienne Rich "The Role of the University: Ivory Tower, Service Station or Frontier Post" by S.E. Luria and Zella Luria "Attitude" by Margaret Atwood
Week 3	Parents and Children	"Once More to the Lake" by E.B. White "Letter to My Mother" by Barbara Kingsolver
Week 4	Life and Death	"Go Gentle Into that Good Night" by Roger Ebert "How the Bean Saved Civilization" by Umberto Eco

Sample 2–This example presents literary non-fiction as historical artefact, demonstrating its importance and evolution over a period of time.

	Topic	Readings
Week 1	Early writers	"Of Cannibals" by Michel de Montaigne "A Modest Proposal" by Jonathan Swift "Of Studies" by Francis Bacon
Week 2	19th Century	"The Death of the Moth" by Virginia Woolf "Self-Reliance" by Ralph Waldo Emerson
Week 3	20th Century	"The Little Store" by Eudora Welty "The Search for Marvin Gardens" by John McPhee
Week 4	21st Century	"Consider the Lobster" by David Foster Wallace A relevant TED talk (some transcripts available online)

Sample 3 – This example looks at non-fiction using some of the elements of fiction, connecting fiction and non-fiction at their most basic levels.

	Topic	Readings
Week 1	Character	"He and I" by Natalia Ginzburg
		"Total Eclipse" by Annie Dillard
Week 2	Setting	"Lonely Places" by Pico Iyer
		"Where the World Began" by Margaret Laurence
Week 3	Point of View	"My Fling with Men's Mags" by Ann Marie McQueen
		"Francs and Beans" by Russell Baker
Week 4	Symbol	"Through the One-Way Mirror" by Margaret Atwood
		"The Temple of Fashion" by Joyce Nelson

Getting Started

As with Short Fiction, you may wish to introduce this new genre by asking students to complete a Self-Reflection Questionnaire. After the section is completed, they may do another reflection to see if their initial impressions have changed at all (see Appendix 1).

Once students have considered what they already know about non-fiction, it may be helpful to define literary non-fiction and then ask students about their notions of argument. Students may identify several types of argument, including those in social media, in order to formulate ideas about presenting an effective stance. What types of arguments do students find convincing? What sorts of arguments encourage listening/reading, and which sorts put listeners/readers off?

This initial exchange can lead to introduction of the basics of rhetorical argument: the three devices that can be used to convince readers that an argument is sound.

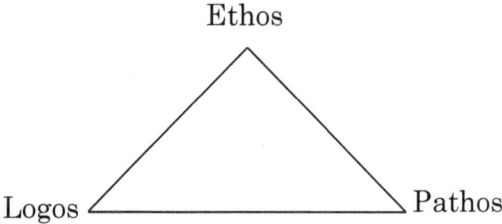

In order to demonstrate these rhetorical devices, it can be helpful to call in visual aids. Show students some advertising taken from magazines or online. Ask them to describe the type of rhetorical device being used. For example, an ad that promotes a product because "four out of five doctors recommend it" is using ethos, trying to convince the audience through authority. An ad for an animal shelter showing a maltreated dog is using pathos or emotion. This is a simple visual exercise, but it helps to reinforce what may be harder to notice in written words.

In all forms of persuasive non-fiction, the author attempts to convince the reader that the argument is worth considering.

Non-Fiction

In literary non-fiction, the rhetoric may be subtler since the 'fictional' elements may distract from the rhetorical elements. Students need to be aware of and point out both the fictional elements and the argument.

> Teaching ethics requires students to encounter discomfort in light of their beliefs and actions. My task as the instructor is to enable students to consider this discomfort, not as an embarrassing consequence of their reasoning, but rather as a moment to let go of something morally and intellectually unhelpful, and in its place, inspire a sense of curiosity and optimism. It is erroneous to assume that human nature is unchangeable and therefore not worth the effort to analyze; it is the hope in humanity that makes us uncomfortable because we risk becoming disappointed at every turn. Each ethics class is a chance for participants to challenge this discomfort and imagine better ways of living life well. Talking our way through consequences, real and hypothetical, as well as rational and absurd, encourages students not to give up because they are uncomfortable, but to try harder to understand the causes and possible solutions to our moral disquiet.
> Alanda Theriault

In-Class Assignments and Discussion Ideas

1. Ask students about how we are regularly exposed to persuasion and how it 'plays' on our emotions. Discuss potential bias in advertising, elections, news reporting. How does critical reading help us as consumers and citizens?

2. Reading versus hearing: Consider comparing the text of a speech with a recitation of the same speech. For example, Martin Luther King Jr.'s famous "I have a dream" speech has one impact when read and another when heard. Before listening to King's speech, have students read the text, making note of the words they find important. Then, listen to the speech and note differences. Pay attention to sound – the repetition of language and sound and how it influences response. Which elements are most persuasive and why?

3. Ask students to construct a verbal argument responding to a piece of literary non-fiction. Have them 'break down' one of the class readings – what points does the author use? How does the author build the argument? Now, ask the students to consider their construction of an argument in response – which points would they respond to? Which points would they begin and end with? Why? Ideas for response construction may be built in groups and then shared with the whole class. Assessing the strength of each response together may reinforce for students the components of persuasive argument. Group discussion of individuals' work may also emphasize the importance of tact and careful wording during assessment.

Writing Assignments

1. Have students write about an event that stands out in their lives. It can be very minor. Consider facts/logos (place, date), narrative voice/ethos, and emotional response/pathos. Before they write out the event, they need to consider these three points and how they will incorporate them into the text. Then, they are to write about that event in a personal narrative. Finally, they are to consider how personal history also has a point; what can be drawn/learned by the reader from the narration of this event? What contemplation does the writer want to encourage in the reader? What will the reader take as the author's stance?

2. Using one of the works read in class, have students analyze its rhetorical devices. Also, ask them to consider how the work incorporates elements normally associated with fiction writing (e.g., narrative voice, symbols, setting, language). Students may then develop a full written response to the stance taken in the work. Particularly if this assignment follows the warm-up discussion of response construction mentioned above, students may develop confidence in their ability to write analysis and critical response.

The Novel

The Novel

The novel is defined as a fictional prose narrative of considerable length and complexity. As a genre, the novel is no longer 'novel'; as readers we are familiar with its traditional structures and devices. But it has certainly undergone radical transformations since Defoe wrote *Robinson Crusoe*. In the electronic age, it is possible to write (and read) novels on Twitter, with installments appearing each day. Like Dickens' novels, which appeared in monthly installments to eagerly waiting readers, these new novels incorporate traditional forms of storytelling with modern technology. While this abbreviated form of novel writing may be innovative, it does not provide the reader with a prolonged and layered reading experience which the traditional novel, that piece of prose "of considerable length and complexity," does. For this reason, we introduce novels of traditional length and form to our first-year students.

When approaching the design of a first-year course, instructors might wish to consider current high school practices in their regions. What novels are generally taught to students? How are novel studies incorporated in the English curriculum? As we have spoken with many students in first-year university English courses across many years, we have learned that their exposure to novel reading is varied. Some do not study the novel at all in high school, while many read perhaps one novel and state that analysis is plot/comprehension-driven. As Robert Scholes states, however, "reading is not simply consumption but a productive activity, the making of meaning" (8). We try to reach beyond plot knowledge in our teaching of the novel and encourage students to develop active reading, analytical, and writing abilities.

Choosing Reading Selections

Since anthologies do not include novels, you are unrestricted in what you can choose to teach for this genre. While this freedom is liberating, it can also be daunting to make a selection. What to choose? Do we select a novel we personally love to read? Do we pick a classic that students 'should' read?

1. If you divide the weeks of teaching evenly among the six genres in a full-year introductory course, roughly four weeks is given to each. In four weeks, a novel needs to be read, analyzed, and written about. Thus, length is an important issue to keep in mind when selecting a book.

2. Shorter novels which may immediately come to mind (*Frankenstein, Heart of Darkness, The Portrait of Dorian Gray*) may be the perfect length, but the amount of historical background and aesthetic appreciation required can exceed syllabus space. Often, the novel *To Kill a Mockingbird* is taught in high school; a great novel about growing up and coming to terms with self, the book also requires instruction in the history of racism in the southern United States.

3. One of the most common complaints of students about novel studies in high school is that the books did not deal with people their own age in circumstances to which they can relate. While we do not espouse the 'dumbing down' of material simply to engage students, we do try to select novels that are relevant and readily accessible to first-year students. Careful selection of an interesting novel can increase the likelihood of reading compliance as well as engagement with discussions and writing assignments.

4. There are benefits and deterrents to teaching a novel that students have studied previously:

The Novel

a. Revisiting a text already read by students can provide some security for them in the fact that it is not new. Expanding existing ideas and analysis might help them re-evaluate the book and consider it in broader contexts.

b. Revisiting a book they might not have enjoyed, however, might be a form of torture. Turned off by the text once, they may be reluctant to re-read it or feel that first-year university studies ought to offer fresh, more mature material.

Syllabus Ideas

Sample 1 – Richard Wagamese's *Medicine Walk* (2014) is used as an example of teaching a genre based on the elements of fiction.

	Discussion Topics
Week 1	**Setting** – the farm, the mill town, the forest
Week 2	**Characters** – fathers, sons, and mothers – the importance of family, forgiveness
Week 3	**Symbol** – Story as culture, as history, as expiation – the physical book and the oral story
Week 4	**Theme** - Is this an indigenous story or is there a universal theme? What does Franklin discover at the end?

Sample 2 – Bram Stoker's *Dracula* (1897) is a classic novel that does not require much historic background for its enjoyment and analysis. A connection in the film unit could be made with a movie like *An Interview with a Vampire* (1994) or *Bram Stoker's Dracula* (1992).

	Discussion Topics
Week 1	**Form** – letters, diaries, doctor's reports – different voices providing the complete story
Week 2	**Characters** – who is the hero? Is it Mina, Harker, Van Helsing? How does the monster represent the aristocracy (the parasitic aristocrat)? Look at modern images of the vampire in film (*Nosferatu*, Bela Lugosi, *Twilight*)
Week 3	**Setting** – the contrast of busy, industrial, modern London with primitive Transylvania. The typewriter, steam train, legal system versus horses, superstition and drafty castles
Week 4	**Symbols** – flies, fangs and stakes, sleepwalking, white and black

Sample 3 – Miriam Toews' *A Complicated Kindness* (2004) introduces a 16-year-old protagonist who struggles with issues of culture and belonging.

	Discussion Topics
Week 1	The title: straightforward vs. complicated kindness Narrative: Naomi the narrator, letters, stories Toews' style and tone Allusions and symbols in the novel Mapping of characters and major plot events

Week 2	Characters' perceptions of reality
	Introduction of literary criticism on the novel
	Contrasts, contradictions, conflicts, and confusion
	Introduction to writing an essay about the novel
Week 3	Cultural concepts: the Mennonites
	Islands
	Other geographical locations
	Guidelines for construction and submission of the essay
Week 4	Travel and escape
	Climax and conclusion
	Concepts of love and kindness
	Musical allusions
	Planning and drafting the essay

Teaching Tips

1. Discussion of the multiple layers and devices used in a novel presents an opportunity to introduce writing about the novel: an interview with the author, a straightforward piece of literary criticism, or a discussion of an issue addressed within the novel may supplement discussions and introduce students to the contextualization of individual literary works.

2. Introduction to writing academic literary essays is important within the introductory course, and the novel presents an ideal focus for students' first full-length paper essay. Creating a novel-specific topic or group of topics (ideally drawn from class discussions) is usually helpful to students and may discourage unoriginal work. Discussing academic essay writing in each class can help to guide students through their writing processes; small assignments may be submitted as well to provide feedback as students develop their essay ideas for their arguments. Expectations for this first academic paper in English should be controlled, as many students will never have written an argumentative essay prior to this course.

Getting Started

As with the other genres, asking students to complete a Self-Reflection Questionnaire may help them to focus and consider their prior knowledge and beliefs about the novel. After the section is completed, they may do another reflection to see if their initial impressions have changed at all (see Appendix 1).

As a way of establishing context, it may be useful to begin discussion by comparing and contrasting short and long fiction. This may also be a good time to mention types of non-fiction often written to explore novels, particularly if you plan to use interviews, criticism, etc. to supplement discussions. The idea of literary conversations may appeal to students, as they often find it interesting that works are never written (or read) in isolation. Broadening one's perspective of a novel, for example, may open doors to participating in conversations among diverse authors and readers.

> Although novels can introduce readers to new and interesting historical contexts, social relationships, among other features, it can be difficult for students to locate themselves within or in relation to their texts. Every reader, however, has a place within the novel, a role which brings to life the words on the page. I find it useful for students to orient themselves early and build their reading experience from there. Perhaps that means stopping at the end of the first paragraph, or the first sentence, and asking oneself a few questions. Where am I? Who is the one talking? And are they talking to me? If answers to those questions are not evident then continue to read until they become clear. Experienced readers will find it easier to visualize and step into a world or mind outside their own, but for beginning literary scholars, for those unsure of what move to make first, it's helpful to begin with what's most familiar: themselves.
>
> Jeremy Johnson

You may wish to assign the entire novel as a reading for the first class or break it up into chapters to be read for each class in the section. Advantages to asking students to complete the entire novel include the ability to discuss the whole plot and all the characters on the first day (without giving anything away). As we emphasize that comprehension of the plot is only the first step in reading a novel actively, the sooner the plot can be mapped, and the characters can be identified, the better. Taking a small amount of class time to do this allows students to clarify their comprehension and/or may provide motivation for those students who have not completed the novel in time for the initial discussion.

In-Class Assignments and Discussion Ideas

The following suggestions can be used as discussion starters or as ideas for short in-class written responses.

1. The opening sentence of any novel is important; it grabs attention and prepares the reader for what is to come. Have students look at opening sentences of novels and talk about what they reveal:

> a. "It was the best of times, it was the worst of times, it was the age of wisdom, it was the age of foolishness, it was the epoch of belief, it was the epoch of incredulity, it was the season of Light, it was the season of Darkness, it was the spring of hope, it was the winter of despair…" (*A Tale of Two Cities*)
>
> b. "It was a bright, cold day in April and the clocks were striking thirteen." (*1984*)
>
> c. "'Where's Papa going with that ax' said Fern to her mother as they were setting the table for breakfast." (*Charlotte's Web*)
>
> d. "Mr. and Mrs. Dursley were proud to say they were very normal thank you very much." (*Harry Potter and the Philosopher's Stone*)
>
> e. "Call me Ishmael." (*Moby Dick*)

f. "Later, as he sat on his balcony eating the dog, Dr. Robert Laing reflected on the unusual events that had taken place within this huge apartment building during the last three months." (*High-rise*)

g. "There was a hand in the darkness, and it held a knife." (*The Graveyard Book*)

h. "It is a truth universally acknowledged, that a single man in possession of a good fortune, must be in want of a wife." (*Pride and Prejudice*)

2. A good cover is often a reason for our picking up a book. What does the design of a cover prepare readers for between the covers? Consider:

a. Texture of paper (some publishers use smooth, glossy stock while others are rougher in texture)

b. Image on the cover (A piece of art? A graphic? Only text? Does specific image use imply scholarly or mass publication?)

c. Paperback or hardcover (is there a disposability in a paperback?)

d. What about digital books? Does the turning of a physical page and the turning of a digital page have the same feeling? Does the size or weight of a tablet versus the size and weight of a book also affect how we feel about our progress through a book? Is there an impermanency suggested in a digital book or do we have two libraries – one online and one that is on shelves?

3. Unlike short fiction which often does not allow for great development of character, a novel allows a writer to explore character transformation. Have students map out character evolution over the course of the novel. In *A Complicated Kindness*, for example, some characters' lack of evolution influences the growth of other characters.

4. Connected with character is also discussion of hero/protagonist and villain/antagonist. In a novel like *Dracula*, the hero and villain are obvious. In much modern fiction, the protagonist is often his or her own worst enemy.

5. Setting can be mapped, encouraging students to consider physical location and its connection to both the plot and to character development. For example, in *Medicine Walk*, the protagonist moves from farm, to mill town, to a journey through the British Columbia forests.

6. If there is a film version of the novel, it might be useful to view it once the novel discussion is complete. Did the film alter any of the book or did it maintain plot elements? Did choice of actor alter perceptions of the character? A caveat or two here, though: students may view watching a film in class when they have already read the novel as wasted time and may not attend. Also, it may be difficult to allot class time for watching the film version when discussion of the novel is already limited in the syllabus.

Writing Assignments

1. Assigning a significant paper at this point in the semester may be reasonable, but students will likely need to be guided through the layered writing processes involved. As mentioned in the Considerations chapter, dividing the assignment into steps may help students understand its complexities. You may wish to assign a personal essay, a compare/contrast essay, a researched essay – the form should be consistent with departmental requirements so that first-year students may become familiar with expectations for academic writing in your institution. Breaking the assignment into two or three steps will give you the opportunity to evaluate students' understanding and progress as well as give students the opportunity to earn marks for process as well as final product. Acknowledging students' learning processes as well as their developing writing processes at this point is critical;

being patient with them in their first year is an investment in their developing academic abilities and confidence as they progress through their studies.

2. Another approach to writing during the novel study is to include non-evaluated assignments in which students write responses to the novel, critical works, or responses to discussions. These may be done in class, or they may be cumulative and submitted as a journal assignment for completion credit only. Some instructors feel that being asked to write about literary works without the pressure of detailed evaluation helps students learn more quickly to express their ideas clearly and freely.

3. As mentioned earlier, it is also possible to design portfolio assignments for an introductory course. As students complete each assignment during the term, they are asked to put it into their portfolio. The assignments may then be evaluated as a group, and marks may be given for progress in designated areas of priority (e.g., clarity, sentence structure, organization of argument, etc.). Submissions may be as frequent as you wish, or portfolios may be submitted once a semester. Students with whom we have worked have appreciated more frequent submission of assignments so that they develop a sense of 'how they're doing' in the course. The earlier in a semester that students receive feedback on their writing, the sooner they can begin to learn and improve.

Poetry

Poetry

At university or college, we tend to tell our students that they must write with clarity and with meaning. Ambiguity is to be avoided at all costs. A logical question would then be, "Why teach poetry, a genre generally associated with ambiguity and emotion, not with logic?" In the 21st-century, when information is only an 'enter' key away, this genre might appear to have less relevance than prose. It is not the medium for conveying information; instead, it is associated with the expression of personal revelation, pain, love, fear, heartbreak – in short, it is the medium for conveying emotion. In ancient times, it was the medium for storytelling with the great epics of Homer, *Beowulf*, and *The Divine Comedy*. However, statistically, poetry is the form of expression most often turned to in times of personal or national crisis. The number of poetry collections about war speaks to this importance of poetry during times of crisis. In recent history, in the aftermath of the 9/11 terror attacks, "people turned to poems when other forms failed to give shape to their feelings" (Metres 219).

Why then do many students have such a hard time with this genre? One of our students described poetry as 'the math of literature'. It had too many rules and required too much thought in order to decipher it; all pleasure was destroyed in the mental work. This is the attitude that instructors need to address.

First-year students generally report that they have had very little formal poetry instruction in their upper years of high school. Poetry is included in the curriculum content, but the skills needed for thoughtful analysis are often not honed.

Teaching Tips

1. Like all the genres, this one has the connecting elements of
- Setting
- Character
- Voice
- Symbol
- Theme

Using these elements may help you start the selection process and the organization of your syllabus section on poetry. The elements may also be used to connect a few poems to other works analyzed during the course. Students may appreciate being able to recognize familiar elements in a genre with which they may not be as comfortable.

2. The one major difference between prose and poetry is, of course, form. It just *looks* different on the page. The poet chooses how to construct the work visually; line breaks are made specifically for both visual effect and meaning. Think about comparing poetry to other art forms like photography or painting. As viewers of the visual arts, we have to 'read' a work in order to understand it. This will also be important in the film section.

3. Also with respect to form, poetry has many: sonnet, ode, elegy, epic, haiku, sestina, pastoral, dramatic monologue, limerick.... For a first-year student, recognizing and understanding all of these forms can be overwhelming. It can also be unnecessary at this stage. For students who will not be English majors, being able to recognize the difference between all types of poetic forms is pointless; students who will continue to study English will learn more about various forms as they advance in their education. Choosing one or two poetic forms to look at may help students appreciate form and see how it works with expression; if students are introduced to too many forms, they may become overwhelmed and not grasp its purpose in poetry. Sonnets work well because the form can be fairly obvious and

straightforward; once students work with sonnets, they can move to other forms and look for connections between those forms and poetic expression.

Here is some terminology, relevant to form and expression, that should be introduced:

- Narrative versus lyric
- Line
- Rhyme
- Meter
- Stanza
- Simile, metaphor, personification
- Enjambment

4. Attempting to provide an overview of the history of poetry may not be as effective as introducing a few key principles of reading poetry and encouraging students to become comfortable with them during the few short weeks available in the course.

Choosing Reading Selections

1. With a plenitude of poetry to choose from, the question is, once again, where to begin? Some anthologies give an historical overview, beginning with works by Chaucer and working their way through the centuries to the modern era. Again, you need to think about what this course is designed to do. If your English degree program offers an historical/literary survey course (usually in 1st or 2nd year) on the history of the English canon (what we like to call the "Beowulf to Virginia Woolf" course), this historical overview will be covered. English students will also get more intense exposure to specific historical periods and authors in upper-year courses. In general, the 1st-year genre course is meant to expose students to each genre and have them come to terms with detailed analysis of text.

2. So then, where to start with selections, if not historically? Consider providing a selection of voices (male, female, cultural) and poems that are light hearted or immediately appealing for other reasons. You may wish to limit selections to those with open or closed form (see Syllabus Ideas, Sample 1) those that share similar themes (see Syllabus Ideas, Sample 2), or those that have visual or dramatic appeal (see Syllabus Ideas, Sample 3).

Syllabus Ideas

Sample 1 – This example looks at poetry based on **form** (closed form, with the sonnet as the specific example, and open form).

	Topic	Readings
Week 1	What is poetry? Ways to read poetry What is an explication?	"Poetry" by Nikki Giovanni "Poetry" by Marianne Moore "How to Read a Poem: A Beginner's Guide" by Pamela Spiro Wagner
Week 2	**Closed form** Example of closed form: the sonnet – why a poet might use a specific form Diction, personification, symbol	"My mistress' eyes are nothing like the sun" and "Shall I compare thee to a summer's day?" by William Shakespeare "Death, be not proud" by John Donne "Shakespearean Sonnet" by R.S. Gwynn

Week 3	**Open form** Example of open form: dramatic monologue (poetry as theater) Voice, setting Some others - are these really poems?	"My Last Duchess" by Robert Browning "The Colonel" by Carolyn Forché "I(f)" by e.e. cummings
Week 4	**Slam poetry** – the role of poetry in the 21st century. Hearing poetry; poetry as a living 'thing'	YouTube video "We Belong Here: Poetry and the Spoken Word"

Sample 2 – This example is based on a **theme** (identity in America) and would tie in (thematically) with works in the other genres.

	Topic	Readings
Week 1	A discussion about poetry – what it is, why people would read or write it, how to read it	Essay: "Beyond Grief and Grievance: The Poetry of 9/11 and its Aftermath" by Philip Metres (online at poetryfoundation.org) "Poetry" by Nikki Giovanni
Week 2	**Closed form**: The sonnet	"Amoretti: Sonnet 37" by Edmund Spenser "Ozymandias" by Percy Bysshe Shelley "The New Colossus" by Emma Lazarus

Week 3	**Open form**	"Marriage" by Marianne Moore (just the first 25 lines) "Ellis Island" Joseph Bruchac III "Theme for English B" by Langston Hughes
Week 4	**Poetry as performance** – the oral tradition Poetry as essay Poetry in song	"3 Ways to Speak English" TED Talk with Jamila Lyiscott (a spoken essay poem) Lyrics to "America" by Simon and Garfunkel

Sample 3 – This example looks at the **visual/dramatic aspects** of poetry, connecting it with drama and film. *

	Topic	**Readings**
Week 1	A discussion about poetry – what it is, why people would read or write it, how to read it (visual form indicates reading)	"Fog" by Carl Sandburg "Shall I compare thee to a summer's day?" by William Shakespeare

Week 2	Poetry as visual image	"Facing It" by Yusef Komunyakaa "Hawk Roosting" by Ted Hughes "The Shark" by E.J. Pratt
Week 3	Poetry and the senses	"Pumpkins" by Tim Lilburn (sound) "Dark Pines under Water" by Gwendolyn MacEwan (sight) "War Movie in Reverse" by Mark Johnston (touch) "Blackberry Eating" by Galway Kinnell (taste)
Week 4	Contexts – poetry as an expression of experience: war, male and female perspectives; civilian and soldier	"And Still I Rise" by Maya Angelou "The Bombing of Baghdad" by June Jordan "Dulce et Decorum Est" by Wilfred Owen

*Specific connections between poetry and drama or film may also be made: For example, Langston Hughes' "Negro" or "Harlem" would work well with August Wilson's "Fences."

Getting Started

As with the other genres, ask students to complete a self-reflection on their prior knowledge and beliefs about poetry. After the section is completed, they may do another reflection to see if their initial impressions have changed at all (see Appendix 1).

> One thing I tell my students all the time: don't worry at first about what a poem *means*. Meaning is only one of the things that a poem does while it's moving down the page. Instead ask, "What does the poem *do?*" This allows us to start off with some simple answers like, "It uses regular stanzas," or "It describes a scene with birds in it." That focuses us right away on the pleasures a poem provides. We don't watch an accomplished dancer and ask ourselves, "What does that dance mean?" We don't look at a painting and worry at first, "What is the meaning of that colour choice?" We might do some of that later, but our first response tends to be, Wow. Poets want that same Wow.
>
> Adam Sol

When the self-reflection has been completed, introduce a general discussion of poetry that includes the following questions:

- Ask students general questions about their comfort with reading poetry. Do they like reading poetry? If not, why not? Do any of them write poetry?

- Ask them if they have a favorite song whose lyrics really interest them. How are song lyrics different from poems? Let them know that ancient poets would have sung their poems, so poetry has a long association with music.

- Ask why we grow out of poetry – after all, we grow up listening to or reading poetry as children. At what stage do

Poetry

we grow away from it? Why is poetry seen as either childish or super intellectual?

In-Class Assignments and Discussion Ideas

The following suggestions can be used as discussion starters or ideas for short in-class written responses.

1. At the start of each poetry class, divide the class into small groups (groups of four is a good number if you have a large class). Make a copy of a poem that they have not previously read. It can be from the anthology or find something unusual online. We have used E.J. Pratt's "The Shark," Marilyn Dumont's "How to Make Pemmican," and Donna Stonecipher's "Model City [4]". Give the groups five minutes to work on the poem – what is the imagery; what is the tone; what "story is being told"? Then, have students present their findings. Working as a group may help those reluctant to speak in class more willing to contribute their thoughts and impressions. Even with a tight deadline of 5-10 minutes, students often are able to come up with very good insights into the poem.

2. Ask students to read a poem out loud. Read the poem several times with each student reader putting emphasis on different words. How does the reading change the poem? You may wish to focus on one line or even one word in the poem and consider various readings that influence meaning. For example, in Marilyn Dumont's poem "How to Make Pemmican" (which is basically a recipe for pemmican that begins with the wonderful line "Kill one 1800 lb. buffalo"), the final line is just "mmmh." Is this the sound of anticipation for the finished product? Is it the sound of memory for the traditional dish? Is it the sound of cultural confrontation – after all, how does one even go about killing an 1800 lb. buffalo? All three readings give a different meaning to the poem.

3. YouTube has many poetic readings of famous poems. Ask students to listen to a poem they prepared for class. How does listening to it change their experience with the poem? This ties in well with discussions about drama.

4. If dramatic monologues are read, ask students to act out the poems. For example, if Browning's "My Last Duchess" is read, ask students to think about the poem as a play; dialogue is already provided so they must design a set and provide character motivation and description.

Writing Assignments

In addition to the above ideas which can be converted into more formal writing prompts, here are some suggestions for writing assignments:

1. Poetry connects well with the visual arts. Ask students to provide an explication of a specific poem. Be sure you provide a clear explanation of what an explication is. We often hand out an example for them, so they can see the kind of detail that is expected. Once they complete the explication, ask them to compare the poem thematically with a piece of art you have selected. Art needs to be 'read' just as a poem needs to be 'read', looking for clues as to meaning. The following are just a few that work well together:

    a. Arthur Smith's "The Lonely Land" and Frederick Varley's "Stormy Weather"

    b. Wilfred Owen's "Anthem for Doomed Youth" and Alex Colville's "Infantry, near Nijmegen, Holland"

    c. Walt Whitman's "When I heard the Learn'd Astronomer" and Van Gogh's "Starry Night"

Poetry

2. Do several in-class explications over the weeks spent on poetry. Start with a simple and short poem to build confidence and progressively make the poems more difficult. By doing the explications in class, students won't have on-line resources as recourse.

3. Ask students to bring in their favorite song lyric. Then, ask them to work on the lyric and explicate the songwriter's words in detail.

Drama

Drama

Dramatic works are immediately recognizable because of how they look on a page. Written primarily as dialogue, plays have no narrator to provide interpretation, explanation, backstory, or inner dialogue. Many plays include stage directions describing setting, character appearance, or movement about the stage. This is not always the case, however (Shakespeare being the obvious example), and readers (and actors) are left to imagine these details.

Unlike other prose works, plays are meant to be seen, not read (closet drama being the exception to this rule). Thus, actors and literature students alike must analyze plays and their characters in order to understand character motivation, decide how dialogue would be delivered (which words require emphasis) and 'choreograph' movement around the stage to support dialogue. As such, analysis of a play takes on a three-dimensional quality; we can move from simply reading text to inquiring about body movement, setting, tone, and physical appearance and costume. Thus, readers of plays are essentially involved in the creation of character and setting. As with the other genres, discussion can also include analysis of theme and symbols.

Choosing Reading Selections

1. Most anthologies include a wide variety of plays; almost always there is one of Shakespeare's plays, a classical drama (like *Oedipus Rex* or *Antigone*), something by Tennessee Williams, a translation of one of the great Russian playwrights, and something more modern. This gives you

some range of choice. If you are organizing your syllabus around a theme, time period, nation, or theoretical lens, this will also help shape your selection.

2. Choosing plays to study may appear like an easy task. Anthologies usually include a wide variety of classic and modern plays. We often gravitate to those we feel are canonically important, with the idea that "they should know *Oedipus Rex*" or "*Death of a Salesman* is a modern classic." We also think about our own high school experiences, which probably included at least one of Shakespeare's plays, and assume that our own students will have the same dramatic background. However, this may not be the case for many of your students. There is a current trend in high schools which considers that "traditional classical literature curricula have done more harm than good to so many students over the years" (Gallo 38-39). Some of the logic behind this evaluation of classic plays includes these observations:

> a. Plays usually deal with adult characters (*Hamlet* and *Romeo and Juliet* obviously excluded) who are dealing with adult issues. As Gallo states, "the classics are not about teenage concerns. They are about adult issues" (34).
>
> b. Language is often a barrier to the comprehension of a classic play. Appreciation of the play and its themes cannot be reached until the hurdle of language is overcome and this may take up too much class time.
>
> c. Long plays do not 'grab attention' immediately. Student interest is not captured, and they are unlikely to finish the reading.

Because of this teaching trend, an instructor of a first-year literature course should not assume that all students arrive in the classroom with a certain level of exposure to plays (if any).

Drama

Teaching Tips

1. When selecting plays, as with the other genres, take into consideration the types of students in your classroom and what you want them to 'take away' from the analysis of dramatic works. Will these students go on in English studies or is this an elective course? Will those continuing with English Literature read classic plays in other courses? If so, would the study of other plays in this course be more beneficial?

2. Consider selecting one play that has been made into a film or has been filmed while acted on a stage. After reading and discussing the play, watch the film and consider how medium affects our reaction to the play. This exercise may work well as a bridge between the drama and film sections of the course.

3. One thing you might wish to consider in an introduction to theatre is the use of **micro-plays**. Like micro-fiction, these short plays (only 1 scene which can be acted in 10 minutes) must do a lot in a very short period of time; like poetry, they often use metaphor to extend their meaning and can be surprising or unsettling in their conclusions.

4. Universities may have particular literatures that they would like emphasized in Introduction to Literature courses. For example, Canadian universities might like an emphasis on Canadian writers; the same may apply with American institutions wanting to see a number of American writers included. The study of Indigenous writing may be part of curriculum considerations. When picking a play, take into consideration those institutional interests.

Syllabus Ideas

Sample 1 - This example works through drama as tragedy and comedy, using micro-plays, one-act, and four-act plays.

	Topic	Readings
Week 1	How do plays work? Character Setting Staging	"Applicant" by Harold Pinter "Post-Its (Notes on a Marriage)" by Paul Dooley and Winnie Holzman
Week 2	Tragedy – what is a tragedy? Why would we want to watch tragedy?	*Hamlet* by William Shakespeare*
Week 3	Comedy – what is comedy?	"Sure Thing" by David Ives
Week 4	Monologue – how does a simple dialogue work as a play?	"Rodeo" by Jane Martin

*made into a film

Sample 2 - These plays deal with the concept of 'hero' – the tragic hero and the anti-hero.

	Topic	Reading
Week 1	Introduction to theater and plays. The classic tragic hero	*Oedipus Rex* by Sophocles

Drama

Week 2	The anti-hero	*Death of a Salesman* by Arthur Miller
Week 3	The protagonist as both villain and hero	*Fences* by August Wilson*
Week 4	A play with no hero and no 'action'	"Trifles" by Susan Glaspell

*made into a film

Sample 3 - This example includes some plays that have a similar theme. In this case, the oppression of women in the home is the theme, but an instructor can select from any themes that will connect the plays or connect one play to works in the other genres.

	Topic	**Readings**
Week 1	Introduction to theater and plays. How plays work	"The Date" by Maria Salomon
Week 2	Silence, motherhood, love	"Andre's Mother" by Terrence McNally*
Week 3	The home as prison, female 'jury', male vs female perspective	"Trifles" by Susan Glaspell*
Week 4	Marriage, motherhood, freedom	*A Doll's House* by Henrik Ibsen*

*made into a film

Getting Started

As with the other genres, ask students to complete a self-reflection on their prior knowledge and beliefs about drama. After the section is completed, they may do another reflection to see if their initial impressions have changed at all (see Appendix 1).

> Drama is arguably the most difficult of genres to teach, the most foreign. While a play is, in fact, a story told through the characters on stage, I recommend first telling the students the story of drama. For my introductory lecture, I used Simon Goldhill (*Love, Sex and Tragedy: How the Ancient World Shaped our Lives*), more precisely his framing of the master play Oedipus in his framing of the chapter "The Mother of all Stories: the Greek Oedipus." Imagine this: the Greeks are an ever-growing empire; Oedipus (a foreigner with deformed ankles, an Other) is the saviour of Thebes until he becomes its curse. It is all neatly justified, all for the good of the people. This discourse of praising and blaming those who are different is still with us today, yet we are not much more aware of our own shifting behaviour towards the Other than the ancient Greeks. Ultimately, all the plays, the really good ones at least, deal with an Other (racial Other, gender Other, sexual Other, class Other, disabled Other, and just plain Other – the immigrant and the foreigner). Once students understand that more often than not a play is a commentary on the social, political, and historical contexts, they are much more willing and engaged in understanding plays. From here, all the plays are open: *Henry V*; *Merchant of Venice*; *Mourning Becomes Electra*; *Death of a Salesman*; *Juno and the Peacock*; *Angels in America*. Giving students the tools *before* asking them to read their first play is utterly important. Once they know what to look for and how to interpret the sequence of events and the actions of the characters makes reading (and later seeing) plays a fulfilling activity. The fact that the humour in a comedy derives from it being an upside-down tragedy is a plus.
>
> Cristina Artenie

Once the self-reflection is complete, it may be helpful to begin with a general discussion about what students expect from drama:

Drama

- What preconceived notions do they have about the genre?
- Have they ever read a play before? Do they like reading plays? If they do, why do they like it? If they don't, why not?
- Why would a writer write a play rather than a movie script or a novel?
- Have they ever seen a play acted on stage before? If so, what did they think of the experience? Have they ever acted in plays?

In-Class Assignments and Discussion Ideas

The following suggestions can be used as discussion starters or as ideas for short in-class written responses.

1. Have students read parts of the play aloud in class. The entire play does not need to be read; that may be an act of redundancy since students will have (hopefully) read the play prior to class. However, pick an important scene and ask willing students to read it. Ask them about specific lines – how might they be read different ways? How might that change our reading of the character? For example, in the play *Fences*, the primary character Troy discusses fatherhood with his son Cory (Act 1, scene 3). How can we 'read' Troy's character and what he says to his son if this dialogue is read angrily? What if it is read with a note of bantering humor?

2. Have students think about how character is presented in a play. Normally, in fiction, the reader is given physical descriptions of characters which help the reader form a mental picture as well as a more detailed understanding of the character. Often in plays, little or no detail is provided. Ask students to discuss the physical presentation of character in a play and how that affects the audience's interpretation of both character and action. For example, in *King Lear*, how would our understanding of Lear be affected if he were cast as a hearty, healthy middle-aged man or as a feeble, elderly man? How can his mental, physical and emotional decline be understood in each situation? With the play "Applicant,"

Miss Piff is described only as "the essence of efficiency." What does this mean? How could this abstract description be made physical? In two theatrical adaptations of the play *Fences*, James Earl Jones and Denzel Washington both played Troy. How would the large physical presences of Jones create one impression of fatherhood, while the slighter, softer-voiced Washington create another? How would this selection of character portrayal affect an audience's response to that character?

3. Relevant to #2 is the connection between a play and current social and/or political environments. For example, *Raisin in the Sun* was written in 1959; *Death of a Salesman* in 1949. More than 50 years later, both are regularly performed and are relevant to contemporary political and social issues. Shakespeare's plays continue to be theatrical staples with directors maintaining the dialogue but using modern costuming to illustrate the contemporary relevance of the political and social issues. Ask students to comment on the relevance of an older play to today's political or social climates.

4. If possible, watch a film version of one of the plays read in class. Ask students to discuss how the film version might have altered dialogue or events. How does seeing a play differ from reading it? How does watching an actor move about a stage help to interpret dialogue and add meaning to it? How does the actor interpret a specific scene in a way that students might not have expected? For example, the play "Trifles" has been made into a short film (2009). In the film version, Mrs. Wright is seen and heard; in addition, rooms in the house other than the kitchen are explored. How do these additions alter the play? How is perception of authorial intention altered with these additions?

5. If you use plays which are set in the past, ask students to reflect on their preconceived notions about that period. For example, consider the racism of pre-civil rights United States in *Fences* or women's subordination prior to the feminist movement in "Trifles." Ask students to think of words that describe their attitudes or impressions of

'racism,' 'feminism,' 'the American dream.' Do this before they read the play. After reading the play, ask them to re-examine their word list; did their reading and analysis of the play alter their understanding of the ideas?

Writing Assignments

In addition to the above ideas, which can be converted into more formal writing prompts, here are some suggestions for writing topics:

1. For some plays, 'the medium is the message'. For example, the play "Post-Its (Notes on a Marriage)" is a short, humorous version of the play *Love Letters* (1988) by A.R. Gurney. Ask students to consider the medium of communication – a post-it versus a letter. How does this play modernize communication between people (post-it versus letter)? What does communication on a post-it imply about the importance of the content? If the medium of communication was changed again (e.g., to Facebook, Twitter, text messages), how would students design the play?

    a. This 'modernization' of a play can be done with many plays. If you are teaching a classic play, ask students to think about how they might stage the play in a modern setting. For example, *Romeo and Juliet* does not need to feature the forbidden love of young people; it could be set in a nursing home with the two lovers as elderly residents and their children as the barrier to that love.

2. Using any of the plays read, discuss the modern relevance of the theme. For example, "Trifles" and *A Doll's House* are set in the late 19th century. What is the thematic relevance to a 21st-century audience? *Fences* takes place in the 1950s; does it have relevance now? *King Lear* is set in ancient Briton, but does its theme of political chaos and reconciliation have any modern relevance?

3. Using several plays, ask students to consider a common setting. For example, several of the plays listed in the sample syllabi have a main setting of the home (*A Doll's House*, "Trifles," *Death of a Salesman, Fences*). Using 2 plays, ask students to analyze how each playwright uses that setting to support their theme. How is the 'space' gendered? How does that space describe a specific social class? How do male and female characters act in that space?

4. Using any play read in class that has a surprising, disturbing, unconventional, or unnerving ending, ask students to consider why that ending is unsatisfactory – what is it about that ending that disappointed, disturbed or puzzled them? Next, ask them to rethink the ending, providing what to them would be a more satisfying conclusion. Part of this will also include an analysis of how this ending will change characterization, tone and theme. What gets 'lost' from the original plot? Are there elements that would or should not be changed at all? This exercise works well with tragic plays (e.g., *King Lear, Oedipus Rex* or *Hamlet*) and very modern plays (like "Applicant").

Film

Film

Not every English department includes a film component in its introductory course. Film is not, after all, a print medium, and it requires a different approach and set of terminology for its analysis. However, it is also a form of storytelling, and we have prepared students up to this point to analyze critically how stories are told. Film is simply another method of conveying narrative.

In addition, movies are also a large part of our cultural life, accessible not only in theaters but also on-demand in the comfort of our own homes and on our own schedules. "Publicly and privately," writes Timothy Corrigan, "our lives have become so permeated by the movies that we rarely bother to think carefully about them – and less often, if at all, do we think of writing about them" (2). Instead of ruining the entertaining experience of film, analysis may help us understand why we like movies and what they have to offer us beyond simple entertainment.

Choosing Viewing Selections

1. Many colleges and universities have programs in Media Studies. These programs will educate students fully in film, filming techniques, and all the terminology associated with the genre. In an Introduction to Literature course, we are not required to extend the study of the genre beyond how film tells a story. And this is a good thing since many of us, like our students, are consumers of movies, not creators. However, as instructors of literature, we are well equipped to analyze film as story.

2. As with our prose fiction components, movies include

- Plot
- Character
- Setting
- Narrative viewpoint
- Symbol
- Theme

By using these six elements with which students are already familiar, we can approach film as just another version of storytelling.

Teaching Tips

As with the other genres, the thought of selecting only two or three films can be overwhelming. Here are a few things to keep in mind as you narrow down your choice:

1. Consider how the film will be shown to students; if you have 90 minutes for class time, the film needs to fit within those 90 minutes. There are not many films fitting this rather limited amount of time. How much time will you leave for discussion of the film? If you choose to have students watch a film on their own time, then they need access to it. If your department does not have an on-line film collection, you can use sources like the CBC's National Film Board, or YouTube.

2. A film does not have to be 'arty' or 'highbrow' to have value. A big-budget action film is just as open to study as a smaller budget art film. For example, *Star Wars: A New Hope* (1977) is considered the first 'blockbuster' film. It is also a pastiche of World War II films, Japanese film and Samurai culture, Arthurian legend, and 1950s science fiction film. It invites discussion about cross-cultural influences, and science-fiction and fantasy overlap.

3. Some students may find reading the subtitles of foreign-language films difficult. This does not mean that those films cannot be used; it just means that you may wish to think about how those students can re-watch a film so that all the dialogue can be read at their individual paces.

Film

Syllabus Ideas

Sample 1 – This example looks at a variety of film types, connecting them with material taught in other parts of the course.

	Topic	Film
Week 1	Short film – how story can be told in just a few minutes	The website *Short Film of the Week* is an excellent place to find many short films
Week 2	Documentary – argument presented visually	A documentary that deals with any of the topics in the non-fiction section
Week 3	Action film – the superhero, the villain	*The Dark Knight* (2008)
Week 4	Foreign Film – Lola up against time, a version of *Groundhog Day*	*Run, Lola, Run* (1998)

Sample 2 – This example uses only two films, connected by a common theme.

	Topic	Film
Week 1	Residential schooling, abuse	*Indian Horse* (2017)
Week 2	Hockey – teamwork, discrimination, redemption	Discussion about *Indian Horse*

89

Week 3	Traditions and conflict – sealing and hunting versus conservation, alternate viewpoint	*Angry Inuk* (2017)
Week 4	North versus south, survival of culture	Discussion about *Angry Inuk*

Sample 3 — This example uses several short films associated with literary elements taught in other genres (all films are available through the National Film Board of Canada).

	Topic	Film
Week 1	Imagery and symbolism: collage	*Free Fall* (1964) by Arthur Lipsett - drawn from Dylan Thomas's poem, "The force that through the green fuse drives the flower"
Week 2	Character and point of view	*Oscar* (2016) by Marie-Josee Saint-Pierre – a portrait of Oscar Peterson
Week 3	Plot and Narrative	*Who Are We?* (1974) by Zlatko Grgic - an animated attempt to address Canadian national identity
Week 4	Setting	*Glimpses* (2010) by Jean-Francois Pouliot - A walk through 24 hours in an imaginary city

Film

Getting Started

As with the other genres, ask students to complete a self-reflection on their prior knowledge and beliefs about film. After the section is completed, they may do another reflection to see if their initial impressions have changed at all (see Appendix 1).

> When teaching film analysis, I encourage students to understand that nothing they experience when viewing a film is spontaneous, and that, although everything they see and hear might seem as if it is naturally and organically developing from a unique situation, in fact, what they see and hear has been deliberately constructed through several stages of development and by many different persons. When students recognize this in the films that they view, I next encourage students to ask why the work has been constructed in the way that it has. Why did the cinematographer choose these angles? Why have the actors spoken and behaved in this manner? Why has the editor linked these images together in this sequence? Why has the sound design team emphasized these noises over others? Why has the composer written this style of music? All of these questions come from that first recognition: that films are painstakingly and deliberately constructed.
>
> Peter Babiak

Ask students general questions about why and how they watch movies:

- What kinds of film do they individually like and why?
- What do they expect from film?
- What do they not like when they see film?
- What connections can they see between film and literature?

In-Class Assignments and Discussion Ideas

1. Before watching a commercial film, ask students to look at movie posters or other advertisements for the film. What are their expectations of the film just from the poster? What do they expect in the way of action and character? After the film is viewed, ask students to compare their expectations with

their experiences of the film.

2. After viewing a film, ask students to discuss the following:

    a. Plot – how is the story told – In a linear form? In flashback? Is there a coherent message? Does it challenge your opinions? How does the ending make you feel – happy, depressed, confused, angry?

    b. Character – since the viewer does not have a character's internal dialogue or an omniscient narrator explaining motivation, how do we come to understand a character? How are close-ups of facial expressions used to understand emotions?

    c. Point-of-view – what narrative point of view is given to the viewer? For example, Hitchcock's *Rear Window* (1954) gives us only Jefferies' limited view of his neighbours out his window. We are as limited in our understanding of what is going on as he is.

    d. Setting – how does the setting contribute to the plot as well as to the atmosphere? For example, *The Dark Knight Rises* is set in a Gothic version of New York and largely at night. The darkness of landscape and lighting contributes to the feeling of disorientation and fear.

        • Tied in with setting is costume. What do the actors wear and how does that establish character? For example, Luke Skywalker in *Star Wars* wears a white tunic and pants, reminiscent of a young squire or knight-in-training. Darth Vader is dressed in a Samurai-inspired helmet and cape. The black and white immediately define 'good' and 'bad' as well as experience and innocence.

    e. Sound – just as with poetry where the reader needs to listen carefully to the sound the words make, a critical watcher of film needs to pay attention to sound. An obvious focus is music used to score the film. It can be simple, like the menacing music used to announce the presence of the shark in *Jaws* (1975) or the German techno music that drives the action of *Run, Lola, Run* (1998). Students can consider how music has a relationship to narrative. Do specific characters have a specific musical motif (like in *Star Wars* where Luke, Leia, and Darth Vader have their own musical motifs)?

3. If you use short films, reminders of the short texts used in other genres (micro-fiction, one-act plays, etc.) may lead to discussion of key elements in literary works. Which features are essential to storytelling, particularly in a visual medium? Students' initial ideas may be compared with their impressions after they have viewed several short films.

Writing Assignments

In addition to the above ideas which can be converted into more formal writing prompts, here are some suggestions for writing topics:

1. Have students watch a film adaptation of a piece of literature read in the course. What were visible omissions or additions? Has the film adaptation re-created the main themes and plot elements or has it changed the meaning in some way?

2. If film is the final genre in your course, students may be able to compare films to assigned readings across the genres. For example, they might be asked to compare a poem, a play, and a film about war, emphasizing themes or symbols.

3. As a first step into film analysis, students may be asked to describe in detail a literary element of one of the films discussed in class (e.g., setting). In which ways did the element support or conflict with other literary elements presented in the film? If they had directed the film, what would they have done differently or similarly and why?

Teaching Tips

1. We avoid assigning major research essays at the end of students' first academic year. By this time, most students are exhausted, and some can barely imagine completing the assigned work in addition to preparing for final exams. If film is the final genre of the year, rather than asking students to write a major paper, it may be more effective to assign a shorter piece to synthesize key ideas introduced during the academic year. A major paper may be more suitable for the second genre in the semester, as students will then have more time to prepare, draft, and polish it before submission.

Teaching Fundamentals
of Academic Argument

Teaching Fundamentals of Academic Argument

An Introduction to Literature course is an ideal place to introduce fundamentals of academic argument as it is practised in English Studies. The fundamentals in this chapter have been selected from first-year students' questions: often, they hesitate to raise things they don't know in class, but through discussions during office hours, students have helped us realize some of the information they may need as they delve into academic writing.

5-Paragraph Essays vs. Academic Arguments

Many students may have been taught to write 5-paragraph essays and expect to use that format in academic writing; if so, it is important to explain why academic arguments require an extended format. Using graphics to show the structure of a 5-paragraph essay in contrast to an extended format may be an efficient way to approach this topic.

A diagram similar to this one will show the organization and content of a 5-paragraph essay:

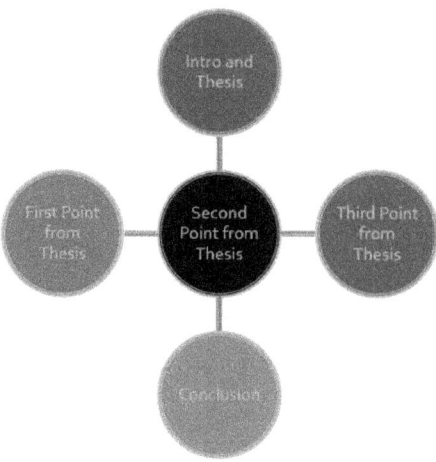

Students should be able to describe the elements of this format and their purposes (they may have seen it depicted as a hamburger previously). They should also be able to share experiences with using this structure that will indicate its pros and cons. Once the need for more complexity and support from expert sources has been established, the need for expanded arguments can be introduced.

Academic arguments may be represented graphically in many ways: following are three representations we have used. In the first example, the thesis is shown as central to the argument, while the introduction, body paragraphs, and conclusion are all linked through a progression of ideas.

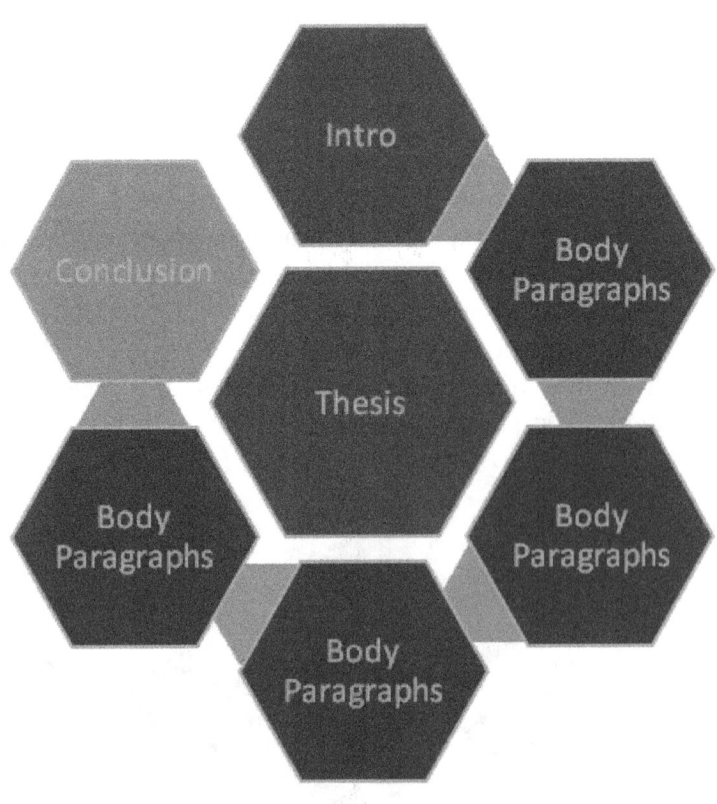

Teaching Fundamentals of Academic Argument

The circular nature of an academic argument is shown in the graphic below, as is the progression from one element to the next:

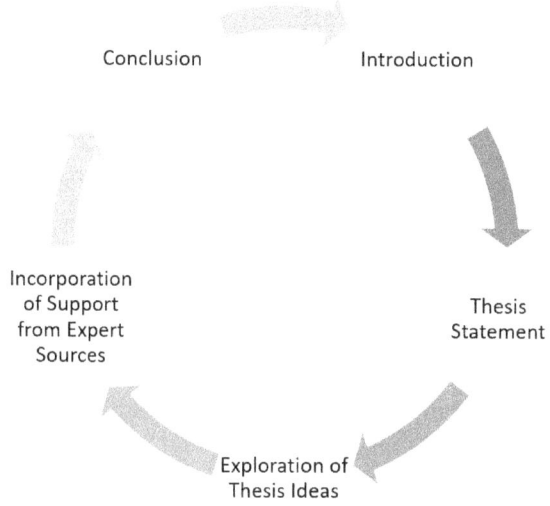

Finally, an academic argument may be compared to the construction of a house in which each component has a specific function and contributes to the over-all solidity of the structure:

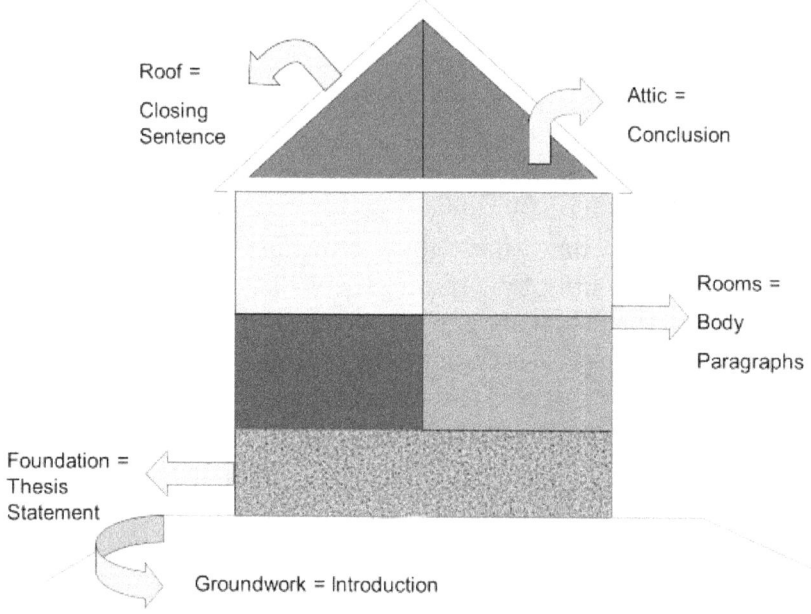

Using an effective visual representation not only will aide introduction of academic argument but will also provide a reference for discussions about writing throughout the course.

Components of an Academic Argument

Students may not be aware that academic arguments are painstakingly constructed; that expressing, explaining, and defending ideas requires skill and extensive practice. They may also feel that they have little to say at first and may benefit from talking about thinking and writing processes. It may feel silly to point out the obvious components of an argument, but in our experience, many first-year students appreciate the details.

A thesis statement...

- is a commitment and an indication of a writer's stance on an issue
- ends the introduction
- often includes an observation plus an answer to "So what?"
- can be agreed or disagreed with
- is broad enough to use as an umbrella for the whole argument, yet specific enough to predict the ideas without listing them
- cannot be the same as an idea from a source!

Instructors may find it worthwhile to teach thesis statements, not only by defining them but also by providing examples of those that are effective versus those not as effective. The following exercise includes weak thesis statements and asks students to improve them; an exercise like this may focus class discussion and encourage students to analyze thesis statements in detail.

Thesis Statement Exercise

The following are attempts at thesis statements. Read each one and indicate what is wrong with the statement. Then, rewrite the statement correcting the errors and making it a better thesis.

1. "*The Great Gatsby* is inarguably the best-written novel of the last 100 years, leaving millions of readers with either a renewed or disenchanted view of the 'American Dream.'"

2. "In his novel *The Long Walk*, it seems as if Stephen King is attempting to make a statement about the evils of laissez-faire capitalism, and in my opinion the characters and settings reflected this well."

3. "In this essay I will try to prove that drugs such as Prozac and Paxil are unnecessary and probably dangerous."

4. There is no question that cell phones have changed our lives in a very big way.

5. The short story "New York Day Women" is about immigration.

6. The iPad has revolutionized the mobile-computing landscape and created a huge profit stream for Apple.

Including thesis statements that are not specifically about literary works is a good way to demonstrate the transfer of writing skills from English Studies to other disciplines.

When developing paragraphs...

- each paragraph should help to explain a sub-topic raised by the thesis and should have a specific purpose
- each topic sentence should indicate what the paragraph is about without saying, "This paragraph will discuss..."

- make sure each sentence has a clear purpose and presents an idea that leads to the next: topic sentence, explanation ("proof") of topic idea through example and analysis (showing connection between evidence and statement), and connection to thesis idea
- if it takes more than one paragraph to show why the topic sentence makes sense, that's fine – begin the second and following paragraphs with a reference to the topic sentence to show that they connect
- quote frequently but briefly from sources to support topic sentences of the paragraphs; introduce all quotations and paraphrases, being sure to indicate where source ideas begin and end; set up and comment on all source material, discussing its meaning or significance to the thesis idea

An introduction...

- guides a reader from a large subject to a specific topic to an issue within that topic
- identifies something the writer has noticed about that issue – an observation
- ends with a thesis statement based on the observation and source content

A conclusion...

- answers the question, "So what?"
- explains how the ideas and examples in the argument work together to support the thesis stance
- ties up loose ends and actually draws conclusions; it does not repeat the thesis statement or summarize the whole argument

Processes of Writing an Argument

Preparing an academic argument involves circular processes rather than a sequence of linear steps. Identifying some of these processes may help students to plan their arguments as well as to set aside more time for writing than they may have in the past. The following processes are essential to the completion of an argument, but they may also be intertwined with others and may be repeated several times:

- Reading assigned literature, related criticism (if used), etc.
- Thinking to write/writing to think: formulating a working thesis statement may help to focus ideas and predict content of the argument
- Organizing: a working thesis statement should indicate major topics in an argument, each topic should indicate ideas for paragraphs, each topic sentence should focus a paragraph and indicate the support and discussion needed to explore it
- Selecting the most relevant literary passages and source material, documenting each selection carefully
- Mapping or drafting the argument before trying to write a complete version
- Clarifying communication details:

    - Accuracy counts and helps to strengthen an academic reputation: does every sentence make a complete point? Is punctuation used correctly? Has enough attention been paid to spell check and have all words with multiple spellings been checked? Have all unintended auto-corrects been caught?
    - Tone: Do all words say exactly what is meant? Is the level of vocabulary appropriate and controlled? Is the tone of the argument professional, yet conversational?
    - Documentation: When students make up their own

styles, instructors notice; use the recommended guide and learn to use it effectively as soon as possible; consider asking for help with documentation at the campus writing center.

Gaining Experience and Improving Argumentation

Sometimes first-year students find writing academic arguments frustrating: we have heard that they are not used to weighing the meaning and value of each word they use, they are not accustomed to having their writing read closely and evaluated, they feel they don't have anything to say, or they are overwhelmed by writing demands. We have also heard from some students that they have always expressed themselves effectively and therefore do not need to adhere to writing conventions. While reinforcing the importance of meeting standards and expectations, we also encourage students to remember that writing well is a life-long process. Wherever they are on the continuum is fine, but there is always room for further development.

Once writing fundamentals are understood and practiced regularly, first-year students may look forward to increasing their arguments' complexities by complicating the evidence they use, incorporating more than one perspective from source material, and strengthening the explanation of their ideas by using clear, controlled language. As they write more frequently, receive feedback, and think about their arguments, they will develop their own writing styles and demonstrate their creativity through varied approaches to topics, incorporation of source material, and expression of ideas.

Sample Arguments

Below we have provided an example of a 5-paragraph essay and an extended academic argument on Charles Baxter's short story, "Gryphon." The discussion in the first essay is limited by the three-body-paragraph structure, whereas in the extended argument, the three points about the main character are used as a springboard for an alternate reading of the story. Using examples like these may help students understand that while 5-paragraph essays are not necessarily immature, they do restrict the possibilities for in-depth academic argument.

5-Paragraph Essay

According to Courtney Summers, "people in a small town feel and look the same" (3). Individuality is more difficult in a community where, in general, everyone knows you, knows your family, and knows your business. Rural communities generally have values which stress hard, manual work and family. Charles Baxter explores this lack of variety in his short story "Gryphon." Set in the 1950s in rural Five Oaks Michigan, the narrator Tommy remembers his Grade 4 teacher, Miss Ferenczi, who brings a bit of excitement to his small town. Her sartorial choices, her refusal to abide by the prescribed curriculum, and her exotic past all intrigue Tommy and vicariously expand his limited creative horizon in Five Oaks.

Sartorial statement is an excellent indicator of character. On her first day of teaching, Miss Ferenczi enters the classroom sporting a purple purse and a checkerboard lunchbox. Both purse and lunchbox – two items held in the hand and presumably of the same size – are distinct in colour and immediately catch Tommy's eye. Her eyeglasses, which she cleans with a "frilly, perfumed handkerchief," have the slightest hint of a blue tint. On her next visit, she is wearing a bright green blouse and pink scarf, a combination Tommy finds hard to keep from looking at. While these items may not appear outlandish, Tommy's remembrance of them implies that women in Five Oaks do not normally sport such bright attire. Flamboyancy and colour are an injection of creative expression into the Grade 4 classroom. Miss Ferenczi's hair and its changing style can also be seen as a creative expression. She first sports a chignon or bun. Its exotic French name indicates "foreignness." Next, she appears in pigtails, a style normally associated with young girls. Finally, her hair is described as disheveled. Our narrator explains that his only reference point for feminine appearance had been his mother, whom he describes as looking like Betty Crocker. Neat, pretty and young, Betty Crocker was the epitome of American domesticity. However, her association with the ideal housewife removes the intrigue of creative expression from the association. In her vibrant, unusual sartorial selection, Miss Ferenczi is the antithesis of the domestic ideal.

The American school curriculum was, for decades, based on rote learning. Multiplication tables, historical facts, and spelling skills were drilled and memorized in primary school. While facts are essential to knowledge, they leave little room for imagination. On her first day of teaching, Miss Ferenczi attempts to stick to the prescribed curriculum, but quickly grows bored with this rigid format and material. Instead, she allows for mistakes, calling them "substitute facts," and suggests that no one "is going to be hurt by a substitute fact." The next day, she begins with a 40-minute monologue of disjointed ideas, some of which have little verity. While there is little factual truth to many of her claims, the children are entranced by the ideas and stories. Finally, her last visit does not even have the pretense of learning. Instead, she begins the class with a tarot reading. The children's teacher has strayed as far from fact and rote learning as possible. While it is arguable that her failure to properly teach could damage the students, Tommy is fascinated by her stories and the possibility of escape for the 'normal' they offer.

Introducing herself to the class on the first day, Miss Ferenczi mentions that she is descended from Hungarian royalty, her mother was a concert pianist and she has lived in some of the great capitals of Europe. For unknown, possibly tragic, reasons, she is now reduced to living in tiny, rural Five Oaks. This social, economic and physical descent down the social scale is tragic, and tragedy is always intriguing. Again, Miss Ferenczi represents an exotic transplant in the mundane life of young Tommy.

In short, the story "Gryphon" presents readers with a teacher who, although she does not teach any verifiable fact, introduces her students to imaginative possibility. For Tommy, Miss Ferenczi has stood out in his memory as an escape from the mundane reality of his small town and his stereotypical family. She represents the magic that may exist outside of Five Oaks, the magic that is represented by the fabulous beast the gryphon.

Baxter, Charles. "Gryphon." *Portable Literature: Reading, Reacting, Writing.* Eds. Laurie Kirszner and Steven Mandell. 9th ed. Cengage, 2016. Pp. 172-187.
Summers, Courtney. *Fall for Anything.* St. Martin's Griffin, 2010.

Thesis-driven Argument

According to Courtney Summers, "people in a small town feel and look the same" (3). Individuality is more difficult in a community where, in general, everyone knows you, knows your family, and knows your business. Rural communities generally have values that stress hard, manual work, and family. Charles Baxter explores this lack of variety in his short story "Gryphon." Set in the 1950s in rural Five Oaks Michigan, the narrator Tommy remembers his Grade 4 teacher, Miss Ferenczi, who brings a bit of excitement to his small town. Her sartorial choices, her refusal to abide by the prescribed curriculum and her exotic past all intrigue Tommy and vicariously expand his limited creative horizon in Five Oaks. However, this can also be read as a tragic story. While Tommy and his classmates are allowed to imagine a fabulous world outside of their little community, Miss Ferenczi is seen as a victim of conformity. She appears to descend into psychological distress as the story progresses. Displaced and alienated, she becomes more fractured mentally until she is expelled from school and, apparently, community.

Sartorial statement is an excellent indicator of character. On her first day of teaching, Miss Ferenczi enters the classroom sporting a purple purse and a checkerboard lunchbox. Both purse and lunchbox – two items held in the hand and presumably of the same size – are distinct in colour and immediately catch Tommy's eye. Her eyeglasses, which she cleans with a "frilly, perfumed handkerchief," have the slightest hint of a blue tint. On her next visit, she is wearing a bright green blouse and pink scarf, a combination Tommy finds hard to keep from looking at. While these items may not appear outlandish, Tommy's remembrance of them implies that women in Five Oaks do not normally sport such bright attire. Flamboyancy and colour are an injection of creative expression into the Grade 4 classroom. Tommy explains that his only reference point for feminine appearance is his mother, whom he describes as looking like Betty Crocker. Neat, pretty and young, Betty Crocker was the epitome of American domesticity. However, her association with the ideal housewife removes the intrigue of creative expression from the association. In her vibrant, unusual sartorial selection, Miss Ferenczi is the antithesis of the domestic ideal.

The American school curriculum was, for decades, based on rote learning. Multiplication tables, historical facts, spelling skills were drilled and memorized in primary school. While facts are essential to knowledge, they leave little room for imagination. On her first day of teaching, Miss Ferenczi attempts to stick to the prescribed curriculum, but quickly grows bored with this rigid format and material. Instead, she allows for mistakes, calling them "substitute facts," and suggests that no one "is going to be hurt by a substitute fact." The next day, she begins with a 40-minute monologue of disjointed ideas, some of which have little verity. While there is little factual truth to many of her claims, the children are entranced by the ideas and stories. Finally, her last visit does not even have the pretense of learning. Instead, she begins the class with a tarot reading. The children's teacher has strayed as far from fact and rote learning as possible. While it is arguable that her failure to properly teach could damage the students, Tommy is fascinated by her stories and the possibility of escape for the 'normal' they offer.

Introducing herself to the class on the first day, Miss Ferenczi mentioned that she is descended from Hungarian royalty, her mother was a concert pianist and she has lived in some of the great capitals of Europe. For unknown, possibly tragic, reasons, she is now reduced to living in tiny, rural Five Oaks. This social, economic and physical descent down the social scale is tragic, and tragedy is always intriguing. Again, Miss Ferenczi represents an exotic transplant in the mundane life of young Tommy.

It is this descent on the social ladder that is the reader's first indication that Miss Ferenczi might be a tragic figure. The family's apparent expulsion from Europe, their destination of Detroit (not New York, Chicago or any of the other great cities of the U.S.), Saginaw (a large industrial city in Michigan) and finally Five Oaks, a small rural community, shows a rapid descent down the cultural, social and economic ladder. If there is any truth in her autobiography, Miss Ferenczi grew up in European cities, was exposed to great culture and was socially superior in her connection to royalty. Not wanting to mix with the other teachers at lunch, preferring instead the company of the students, Miss Ferenczi appears to find no one she considers a peer. Displacement and isolation mark this woman and, in a sense, she becomes the gryphon she has told the students of. Caged, isolated, and on display, Miss Ferenczi becomes a monstrous insertion into small-town society.

Physically, Miss Ferenczi's sartorial choices can also be seen as an indication of mental collapse. Her changing hairstyles can be seen as a creative expression but can also be seen as a deterioration of character. She first sports a chignon or bun. Its exotic French name indicates 'foreignness.' However, it is neat, feminine, and accepted. Next, she appears in pigtails, a style normally associated with young girls. Finally, her hair is described as "appearing hardly to have been combed." Combined with the immediate introduction of the tarot deck and the reading of fortunes, Miss Ferenczi can be seen to have disintegrated physically and emotionally.

The story "Gryphon" presents readers with a teacher who, although she does not teach any verifiable fact, introduces her students to imaginative possibility. For Tommy, Miss Ferenczi has stood out in his memory as an escape from the mundane reality of his small town and his stereotypical family. She represented the magic that may exist outside of Five Oaks, the magic that is represented by the fabulous beast the gryphon. The child Tommy is fascinated by the teacher's sartorial choices, but they do not indicate to his young mind anything about her character other than her distinctiveness among the other women of his limited experience. The reader, however, is able to draw conclusions about her character from the few details Baxter provides. Despite her rather questionable role in the classroom, Miss Ferenczi is a tragic figure, suffering from her isolation in Five Oaks. In the end, she is expelled from the school as teacher and from the community as a person.

Baxter, Charles. "Gryphon." *Portable Literature: Reading, Reacting, Writing*. Ed. Laurie Kirszner and Steven Mandell. 9th ed. Cengage, 2016. Pp. 172-187.

Summers, Courtney. *Fall for Anything*. St. Martin's Griffin, 2010.

Appendices

Appendix 1

This is an example of a simple self-reflection questionnaire that each student can complete before and after each unit. Kept in a portfolio, it can be a measure of student development and engagement over the course.

Self-Reflection Questionnaire (Pre-study and Post-study)

Pre-study

1. How you ever read anything from this genre before?

2. Did you enjoy that reading experience?

3. If yes, why did you enjoy the format of the genre?

4. If no, why did you not enjoy it?

Post-study

1. After reading a variety of material from this genre, how do you feel about it now? Has your opinion changed?

2. What was one thing you learned about the genre that you didn't know before?

3. Was there one piece in particular that you liked? Why?

4. Was there one piece you particularly did not enjoy? Why?

Appendix 2

The following is an example of a syllabus for an academic year. In addition to readings in each genre, topics dealing with writing are included in italics. Mini-lessons on other topics as well as writing assignments (e.g., student journal entries) might be added as time allows.

Term 1	Genre	Topic	Readings
Week 1	**Short Fiction**	**Introduction to the Course** **Character-based stories** – some stories are all about exploring character. Round vs flat; realistic vs caricature; likeable vs disagreeable	"Miss Brill" by Katherine Mansfield "Gryphon" by Charles Baxter "Story of an Hour" by Kate Chopin
Week 2		**Setting-based stories** – some stories explore setting and how it affects plot or character History – understanding the time-period is essential Geography – language, customs, landscape, urban or rural	"Everyday Use" by Alice Walker "New York Day Women" by Edwidge Danticat "The Yellow Wallpaper" by Charlotte Perkins Gilman

Week 3		**Point-of-view stories** First-person, third-person, reliable, unreliable *Thesis statements – the difference between a 5-paragraph paper and a nuanced thesis statement and paper* *Practice exercise*	"The Cask of Amontillado" by Edgar Allan Poe "The Lottery" by Shirley Jackson
Week 4		**Symbol and Theme** Use of symbols Theme – what the author wants us to know beyond the plot.	"Doe Season" by David Michael Kaplan "A Worn Path" by Eudora Welty
Week 5	Non-fiction	**Character** *Introductory Paragraphs - Practice exercise*	"He and I" by Natalia Ginzburg "Total Eclipse" by Annie Dillard
Week 6		**Setting** *Documentation styles: APA, MLA. Practice exercise*	"Lonely Places" by Pico Iyer "Where the World Began" by Margaret Laurence

Appendix 2: Syllabus for an Academic Year

Week 7		**Point of View** *In-Text Citations - how to effectively incorporate and use argument support*	"My Fling with Men's Mags" by Ann Marie McQueen "Francs and Beans" by Russell Baker
Week 8		**Symbol**	"Through the One-Way Mirror" by Margaret Atwood "The Temple of Fashion" by Joyce Nelson

Week 9	**The Novel**: *A Complicated Kindness*	The title: straightforward vs. complicated kindness Narrative: Naomi the narrator, Letters, Stories Toews' style and tone Allusions and symbols in the novel Mapping of characters and major plot events
Week 10		Characters' perceptions of reality Contrasts, contradictions, conflicts, and confusion Introduction of literary criticism on the novel *Introduction to writing an essay about the novel*
Week 11		Cultural concepts: the Mennonites Islands Other geographical locations *Guidelines for construction and submission of the essay*

Week 12		Travel and escape Climax and conclusion Concepts of love and kindness Musical allusions *Planning and drafting the essay*

Term 2	**Genre**	**Topic**	**Readings**
Week 1	**Poetry**	What is poetry? Ways to read poetry What is an explication? *Novel essay draft and/or completed essay may be submitted during this unit*	"Poetry" by Nikki Giovanni "Poetry" by Marianne Moore "How to Read a Poem: A Beginner's Guide" by Pamela Spiro Wagner
Week 2		**Closed form** Example of closed form: the sonnet – why a poet might use a specific form Diction, personification, symbol *In-class explication*	"My mistress' eyes are nothing like the sun" and "Shall I compare thee to a summer's day?" by William Shakespeare "Death, be not proud" by John Donne "Shakespearean Sonnet" by R.S. Gwynn

Appendix 2: Syllabus for an Academic Year

Week 3		**Open form** Example of open form: dramatic monologue (poetry as theater) Voice, setting Some others - are these really poems? *In-class explication*	"My Last Duchess" by Robert Browning "The Colonel" by Carolyn Forché "I(f)" by e.e. cummings
Week 4		**Slam poetry** – the role of poetry in the 21st century. Hearing poetry; poetry as a living 'thing' *In-class explication*	YouTube video "We Belong Here: Poetry and the Spoken Word"
Week 5	Drama	**How do plays work?** Character Setting Staging *Writing an essay on Drama*	"Applicant" by Harold Pinter "Post-Its (Notes on a Marriage)" by Paul Dooley and Winnie Holzman
Week 6		**Tragedy** – what is a tragedy? Why would we want to watch tragedy?	*Hamlet* by William Shakespeare

Week 7		Comedy – what is comedy?	"Sure Thing" by David Ives
Week 8		Monologue – how does a simple dialogue work as a play?	"Rodeo" by Jane Martin
Week 9	Film	**Imagery and Symbolism:** collage *Drama essay draft and/or completed essay may be submitted during this unit*	*Free Fall* (1964) by Arthur Lipsett - drawn from Dylan Thomas's poem, "The force that through the green fuse drives the flower"
Week 10		**Character and Point of View**	*Oscar* (2016) by Marie-Josee Saint-Pierre - a portrait of Oscar Peterson
Week 11		**Plot and Narrative**	*Who Are We?* (1974) by Zlatko Grgic - an animated attempt to address Canadian national identity
Week 12		**Setting** **Course Completion**	*Glimpses* (2010) by Jean-Francois Pouliot - A walk through 24 hours in an imaginary city

Appendix 3

When constructing a syllabus, it is sometimes helpful to choose a few items in each genre that connect thematically. Some discussion can then be had on how writers, within the limits of their chosen genres, convey their perspectives to the reader.

The following are just a few ideas for themes and reading selections that can be included in a syllabus:

Crime, Law, Disorder

Non-Fiction	Martin Luther King Jr "I Have a Dream" Henry David Thoreau "Civil Disobedience"
Short Stories	Shirley Jackson "The Lottery" Conan Doyle "Scandal in Bohemia" Edgar Allan Poe "The Cask of Amontillado" Tobias Wolf "Bullet in the Brain"
Poems	Carolyn Forché "The Colonel" Robert Browning "Porphyria's Lover" Alfred Noyes "The Highwayman"
Play	Susan Glaspell "Trifles"
Film	*Rear Window*

Technology

Non-Fiction	Nicholas G. Carr "Is Google Making us Stupid?"
Short Stories	Ed Park "Slide to Unlock" Amanda Brown "Love and Other Catastrophes: A Mixtape" Lydia Davis "Television"

Poems	Daniel Nyikos "Potato Soup" William Wordsworth "Steamboats, Viaducts, and Railways" Emily Dickinson "I See it Lap the Miles"
Play	Harold Pinter "The Applicant" Paul Dooley "Post-its"
Film	*Imitation Game*

Love and Hate

Non-Fiction	Ralph Waldo Emerson "Love"
Short Stories	James Joyce "Eveline" Kate Chopin "Story of an Hour"
Poems	William Shakespeare "Sonnet 116" John Donne "Valediction: Forbidding Mourning" Elizabeth Barrett-Browning "How Do I Love Thee?" Jeanne Dubrow "Before the Deployment"
Play	Paul Dooley "Post-its" William Shakespeare *Romeo and Juliet*
Film	*Snow Falling on Cedars*

Husbands, Wives, Parents and Children

Non-Fiction	Fran Lebowitz "Children: Pro or Con?"
Short Stories	Edwidge Danticat "New York Day Women" George Saunders "Sticks" Alice Walker "Everyday Use"
Poems	Theodore Roethke "My Papa's Waltz" Julia Alvarez "Dusting" Seamus Heaney "Digging" Adam Sol "Night Driving"
Play	Henrik Ibsen *A Doll's House*
Film	*Away from Her*

Appendix 3: Thematic Readings for a Syllabus

Race

Non-Fiction	Brent Staples "Black Men and Public Space" Binyavanga Wainaina "How to Write about Africa"
Short Stories	Steven Graham Jones "Discovering America" Jamaica Kincaid "Girl" Thomas King "Borders"
Poems	Francisco X. Alarcon "'Mexican' is not a Noun" Gwendolyn Brooks "We Real Cool" Langston Hughes "Harlem"
Play	August Wilson *Fences*
Film	*Detroit*

Imagination and Horror

Non-Fiction	Stephen King "Why We Crave Horror"
Short Stories	Charlotte Perkins Gilman "The Yellow Wallpaper" Shirley Jackson "The Lottery" William Falkner "A Rose for Emily"
Poems	Edgar Allan Poe "The Raven" Samuel Taylor Coleridge "Kubla Khan" Robert Browning "My Last Duchess"
Play	William Shakespeare *Hamlet*
Film	*Pan's Labyrinth*

War and Peace

Non-Fiction	Barbara Kingsolver "A Pure, High Note of Anguish"
Short Stories	Andrée Chédid "Death in Slow Motion" Tim O'Brien "The Things They Carried" Timothy Findley "Stones"

Poems	June Jordan "The Bombing of Baghdad" Wilfred Owen "Dulce et Decorum Est" Thomas Hardy "The Man He Killed"
Play	Shirley Lauro "A Piece of My Heart"
Film	*Full Metal Jacket*

WORKS CITED

Alexander, Patricia A. "The Path to Competence: A Lifespan Developmental Perspective on Reading." *Journal of Literacy Research* 37.4 (2005): 413-36. Web.

Alexander, Patricia A., and Emily Fox. "Adolescents as Readers." *Handbook of ReadingResearch*. Ed. Michael L. Kamil, P. David Pearson, Elizabeth Birr Moje, and Peter P. Afflerbach. Vol. 4. New York: Routledge, 2011. 157-73. Print.

Bazerman, Charles. "Preface." *Genre: An Introduction to History, Theory, Research and Pedagogy*. By Anis Bawarshi and Mary Jo Reiff. West Lafayette: Parlor Press, 2010. xi-xii. Print.

Corrigan, Timothy. *A Short Guide to Writing About Film*. New York: Pearson, 2012. Print.

Côté, James E., and Anton L. Allahar. *Lowering Higher Education: The Rise of Corporate Universities and the Fall of Liberal Education*. Toronto: University of Toronto Press, 2011. Print.

Donald, Janet G. *Learning to Think: Disciplinary Perspectives*. San Francisco: Jossey-Bass, 2002. Print.

Fitzgerald, Tanya. "Scholarly Traditions and the Role of the Professoriate in Uncertain Times." *Journal of Educational Administration and History* 46.2 (2014):207-19. Web.

Foster, Thomas C. *How to Read Literature Like a Professor*. New York: Harper Collins, 2003. Print.

Francis, Michelle A., and Michele L. Simpson. "Vocabulary Development." *Handbook of College Reading and Study Strategy Research*. 2nd ed. Ed. Rona F. Flippo and David C. Caverly. New York: Routledge, 2009. 97-120. Print.

Gallo, Donald."How to Create an Aliterate Society."*The English Journal* 90.3 (Jan. 2001): 33- 39. Web.

Halpern, Diane F. "Teaching Critical Thinking for Transfer Across Domains: Dispositions, Skills, Structure Training, and Metacognitive Monitoring." *American Psychologist* 53.4 (1998): 449-55. Web.

Mann, Sarah J. "The Students' Experience of Reading." *Higher Education* 39 (2000): 297-317. Web.

Metres, Philip. *Behind the Lines: War Resistance Poetry on the American Homefront Since 1941*. Iowa City: Iowa University Press, 2007. Print.

Moje, Elizabeth Birr, Darin Stockdill, Katherine Kim, and Hyun-ju Kim. "The Role of Text in Disciplinary Learning." *Handbook of Reading Research.* Ed. Michael L. Kamil, P. David Pearson, Elizabeth Birr Moje, and Peter P. Afflerbach. Vol. 4. New York: Routledge, 2011. 453-86. Print.

Mulcahy-Ernt, Patricia I., and David C. Caverly. "Strategic Study-Reading."*Handbook of College Reading and Study Strategy Research.* 2nd ed. Ed. Rona F. Flippo and David C. Caverly. New York: Routledge, 2009. 177-98. Print.

Newson, Janice A. "Disrupting the 'Student as Consumer' Model: The New Emancipatory Project." *International Relations* 18.2 (2004):227-39. Web.

Pawan, Faridah, and Michelle A. Honeyford. "Academic Literacy." *Handbook of College Reading and Study Strategy Research.* 2nd ed. Ed. Rona F. Flippo and David C. Caverly. New York: Routledge, 2009. 26-46. Print.

Popovic, Celia, and David A. Green. *Understanding Undergraduates: Challenging our Preconceptions of Student Success.* Oxon, UK: Routledge, 2012. Kobo Edition.

Pugh, Sharon L., Faridah Pawan, and Carmen Antommarchi. "Academic Literacy and the New College Learner." *Handbook of College Reading and Study Strategy Research.* Ed. Rona F. Flippo and David C. Caverly. Mahwah, NJ: Lawrence Erlbaum, 2000. 25-42. Print.

Reason, Robert D., Patrick T. Terenzini, and Robert J. Domingo. "First Things First: Developing Academic Competence in the First Year of College." *Research in Higher Education* 47.2 (2006):149-75. Web.

Roberts, Judith C. and Keith A. Roberts. "Deep Reading, Cost/Benefit, and the Construction of Meaning: Enhancing Reading Comprehension and Deep Learning in Sociology Courses." *Teaching Sociology* 36.2 (2008): 125-40. Web.

Scholes, Robert. *Textual Power: Literary Theory and the Teaching of English.* New Haven: Yale University Press, 1986. Print.

Shanahan, Timothy, and Cynthia Shanahan. "Teaching Disciplinary Literacy to Adolescents: Rethinking Content-Area Literacy." *Harvard Educational Review* 78.1 (2008): 40-59. Web.

Tagg, John. *The Learning Paradigm College.* San Francisco: Anker, 2003. Print.

Taraban, Roman, Kimberly Rynearson, and Marcel Kerr. "College Students' Academic Performance and Self-Reports of Comprehension Strategy Use." *Reading Psychology* 21 (2000): 283-308. Web.

www.ingramcontent.com/pod-product-compliance
Lightning Source LLC
Chambersburg PA
CBHW061958220426
43662CB00011B/1730